About the Authors

MARTIN M. AUZ began his studies in grief recovery in 1978 as an undergraduate. An introductory course, "Death and Dying," introduced him to the works of Dr. Elisabeth Kübler-Ross and piqued his interest in the subject.

Upon graduating from DePaul University, Martin began his career as a marketing director. He later became a freelance writer, contributing to the book *The Orland Story—from Prairie to Pavement,* which was awarded a certificate of excellence by the Congress of Illinois Historical Societies and Museums. In addition, he has authored several articles for specialty periodicals.

Concerned about corporate America's lack of compassion for employees who are struggling with issues of caregiving, death, and grief, Martin conducted extensive research on the subject of organizational grief recovery. The death of his parents less than six months apart in 1997 expanded his interests to include the impact of both the sudden death of a loved one as well as the long-term care of a terminally ill parent.

MAUREEN LYONS ANDREWS is a founder of her local parish's grief recovery program—one of the first in her area. She began her work as a facilitator for the group and coordinated her parish's weekend workshop, "Joyful Again," which dealt with the specific needs and concerns of widows and widowers.

As a chief architect of bereavement programs in the southern suburbs of Chicago, Maureen conducted group support sessions for bereaved families and worked one-on-one with mourners needing additional support. In her work with the elderly, she has learned what issues senior citizens consider to be important with regard to terminal illness and dying: what they fear and what they find comforting. She has counseled various churches and organizations on the proper methods for beginning grief recovery programs and has offered suggestions on how to promote active participation within them.

Maureen has been a panelist at various seminars and workshops on grief recovery sponsored by the Archdiocese of Chicago. She has shared various methods on how the community can help the bereaved. As a direct result of her efforts, today many hospitals, churches, and even funeral homes in the Chicagoland region offer grief counseling, recovery, and support programs.

THIS BOOK IS LOVINGLY DEDICATED

TO THE FOND AND PRECIOUS MEMORIES

OF DAVID LYONS

AND PETER AND ROSALIE AUZ:

OUR TEACHERS,

OUR INSPIRATIONS,

OUR HEART-LIGHTS.

Acknowledgments

WE OWE a debt of gratitude to many people.

To our devoted and supportive families—Sue, Bob, Michael, Keith, Kym, and Kurt—we offer our love and thanks for your constant encouragement, understanding, and assistance.

To the courageous people who allowed us the honor of walking with them through their journeys of grief, we offer our respect and appreciation for sharing your stories.

And to our new friends who are about to begin their journeys through grief, we offer our reassurance and encouragement for a successful and consolatory passage.

Martin M. Auz
Maureen Lyons Andrews
September 29, 2001

Table of Contents

7 SUPPORT GROUPS 123

8 CLOSING THOUGHTS 133

9 OTHER RESOURCES 135

1 | When It Begins

A time for tears,
a time for laughter;
a time for mourning,
a time for dancing.

Ecclesiastes 3:4

DEATH STRIKES. Your life is shattered. Tranquility and order are replaced by chaos and confusion. Yesterday's gone, and it will not return. In its absence, you begin a new and a mysterious journey—a journey through grief.

Death brings a myriad of emotions, responsibilities, and questions to those left behind. Every person faces grief for a first time. Yet even at the dawn of the twenty-first century, nearly half of the adult population has not been involved in planning the funeral of a loved one. And of the 50 percent of people who have planned a funeral, only half of those have planned a funeral more than once. People who have been shielded from death's pain and sorrow not only may be naive and inexperienced with regard to funeral arrangements and grief, but they also may be overwhelmed and tongue-tied. Even people who have had contact with death and grief throughout their lifetime often find that extending condolences to the bereaved can be awkward.

THE HELP YOU NEED RIGHT NOW

Whether it's taking care of a dying loved one, planning the funeral, or learning to cope with the absence of that loved one, grief is the leading emotion. Decisions that must be made in each of these instances—and often in extremely short time frames—may cause confusion and resentment. These are just the first of many byways that must be traveled along one's journey through grief.

We hope this book will benefit the many people who are touched by death. There are those who are facing grief and those who are helping a loved one face grief; those who have never experienced the grieving process and those who have experienced it but are confused or bewildered by the feelings and sensitivities associated with grief. When today's generation meets grief for the first time, the task of finding the right words and actions may seem impossible. In this book we provide suggestions for making this encounter bearable. Some of the information presented will be repeated in various sections, depending upon the particular situation the reader is facing. But each section is structured to offer encouragement to the bereaved and to reassure them that they *will* get past the overwhelming hurt.

We believe that people who are facing the grieving process need help right now. They don't have the time or the energy to delve into books on the meaning, psychology, or theology of grief. They need a point of reference with which to begin, somewhere to find the help they need as they are thrust into this journey.

WHAT THIS BOOK PROVIDES

This book presents basic topics relating to grief. We have provided short descriptions of what to expect, of what you need, and of what others need from you. We have put a lot of information into simple list form, and we have organized all of this in a way that makes the information easy to find.

Sometimes, when a death has been violent or high profile in some way, a person is thrust into the role of being a "grief manager." The grief manager may not actually be one of the bereaved yet is expected to know what to say and do and to give support to the bereaved. Sometimes a support person must leave his or her own grief in the background so that full attention can be given to immediate family members of the deceased. This book provides guidelines for getting through these situations.

We make no attempt to rationalize, analyze, sermonize, or philosophize death, grief, religion, or our own beliefs. We have not presented case studies and examples. These may be found in the works that further explore the many aspects of grief. We are merely presenting ideas and suggestions for coping that we have found beneficial through personal experience, traditional research, and interaction with people in varying stages of the grieving process.

We conclude this work with lists of books to read and organizations to contact for help with the grieving process. They are presented here merely as a catalog of available resources that we have found to be helpful. These lists are not comprehensive but offer a good start for readers who want more information.

It is our hope that this book provides direction for the bereaved, guiding them through the tears and confusion to a place of healing and understanding. At various points in the journey, certain milestones will mark the nearness of their destination: emotional pain will become less severe; physical maladies will start to subside; feelings of being held captive by the memories of the deceased will begin to dissipate. Whether it's the reader's own journey or that of a loved one, this book provides guidelines for dealing with the many emotions associated with grief.

We also hope that this book will give the reader a better understanding of the words, actions, and individual time frames that are required to complete the grieving process. Grief is work. It's painful. You may think you can circumvent it or even ignore it. But if you pack grief away, it only resurfaces in some other aspect of your life. Face grief head-on. It won't be an easy or quick task, but it will help lessen the pain and begin the healing.

Yesterday is gone. Tomorrow is a long way off. But today is here. The hurt is in the present. So today, the journey begins.

2 | What to Do, What to Say

Give sorrow words. The grief that does not speak
Whispers [to] the o'er-fraught heart and bids it break.

William Shakespeare, Macbeth, *IV.iii. 209–10*

ONCE THE ORDEAL of burying a loved one has been completed, those left behind face an entirely new and different life. Whether it's the loss of a spouse, parent, child, or friend, a void now exists where once there was love, friendship, and comfort; a remarkable human being is now gone. Reacting to this void is difficult for the bereaved and for those family members, friends, and coworkers who want to help. Knowing what to do, where to turn, and what to say can be a challenge. Yet we must do our best to bring consolation to those in the depths of heartache and despair.

If you are grieving, don't avoid the pain you feel but begin the healing process now by acknowledging and dealing with it. If you are supporting a person in grief, learn the ways in which you can offer the best help.

WHEN YOU ARE THE ONE WHO IS GRIEVING

Healing from the loss of a loved one takes time. Regardless of whether your family or friends help you with your transition, there are certain things you can do to help yourself progress through the grieving process.

Try to maintain a normal, or lighter than usual, daily schedule and routine.

Your body needs time to reenergize from the grueling task of saying goodbye and burying a loved one. New responsibilities or new environments may only delay your healing. You need some time to grieve. Only by fully experiencing the pain of your grief and working at resolving it can you begin to heal.

Live for now.

Don't live in the past, with its regrets, resentments, and anger. Don't live in the future, with its uncertainty, worries, and fears. Live for today. This is not to say that you should throw out memories of your loved one. Just don't dwell on what was and what might have been. Concentrate on what you have to achieve today. Worrying about what lies ahead is destructive and drains your energy. As you start setting daily goals and achieving them, eventually you can begin developing long-term plans.

Be good to yourself.

Understand that it's OK to feel depressed, to hurt, and to be angry with the deceased, the doctor, the hospital, and even God. It's also OK to go out with friends and have a good time. Enjoy the people who are still in your life. There is no "right" way to grieve—only your way. And there is no set time frame that your grief should follow—only your time frame. There is no fixed period of mourning, no matter what other people may tell you. Be patient. And do not compare how you are grieving with how other people are grieving.

Understand that healing is a process that takes time.

Keep decisions—especially major ones such as selling your house or moving across the country—to an absolute minimum, particularly in the days just after the funeral. Try to allow yourself one year before making these types of decisions. You will be able to think much more clearly at the end of one year than in the days immediately after your loved one's funeral. Keep believing that eventually you will recover from your loss, and you will. But in the meantime, make no snap decisions.

Let yourself cry.

Crying is a release mechanism; it's therapeutic. It serves to help lessen the pain. Go ahead and cry; sob or scream if you need to. You will most likely feel better for doing so. Crying is not a sign of weakness; rather, it shows your love and concern. So, don't prevent yourself from crying, but don't force yourself to cry, either. And never apologize to others for your tears—they belong to you and serve as a release and an expression of your emotions at various stages of your mending process. Looking at pictures of your loved one or visiting the grave might bring tears. But each tear released further opens the heart for healing and allows your journey through grief to progress.

Keep a journal.

Writing down your thoughts and emotions can be very helpful during your sorrow. Use whatever is most comfortable—a paper journal or a computer. Either way, when you read your words later, you will see that your journey through grief is progressing. If you can't keep a journal, at the very least express your feelings verbally. Hearing what you have kept inside will release some frustration and stress and begin the healing process. It will help you accept your feelings—feelings that you did not choose but must deal with nonetheless.

If someone offers to help you in some way, accept it.

Conversely, if family and friends are staying away, not calling or offering assistance, *ask* them for help. Others cannot read your mind. Most people will want to help but may not know what they can do for you. So they may seem passive when actually they are held back by feeling inadequate. Ironically, it will be up to you—the one who needs help—

to somehow lead others and teach them how they can help and comfort you. For instance, you might say, "Keep calling and asking me to meet you for coffee and pie, so that we can talk. I probably won't go, but I need you to keep calling and asking." Eventually, one day, you may actually find that you want that coffee and pie, that you want to talk, and that you want to thank your friend for being persistent!

Attend to your physical needs.

Get enough rest by going to bed early and avoiding caffeine after dinner. Keep yourself healthy by limiting the amount of junk food you eat and by planning daily, well-balanced meals. Avoid alcohol, sleeping pills, and tranquilizers, which could actually be more harmful to you and delay the healing process. Such medication merely camouflages your emotions. Grief is work. It is painful. You need to keep busy. Exercise if possible. Physical activity relieves stress. Even a short walk around the neighborhood will help. And, while it is common to be depressed, guard against totally withdrawing and severing ties with family and friends. This could be a sign that you need professional assistance in dealing with your grief. If any other health problems arise—headaches, difficulty sleeping, loss of appetite—see your family physician for help and advice. Although these are normal reactions to grief, a doctor should be consulted.

Find someone to support you through your grief.

If friends or relatives are available, don't be afraid to ask for their help. All they really need to do is listen and provide some comfort. It's OK to need comforting, and it's always advisable to have someone help you with your grief journey. At first, those closest to you will be your strengths. But, because they may not understand that grief work takes time, they might encourage you to "get on with your life." That is when it might be advantageous to seek someone outside of your family or circle of close friends who is willing to help you with your grief process. If personal acquaintances are unavailable, clergy or support groups can help. At the very least, read books on grief. There are numerous books available that can help you understand what you are going through and that you are not alone in facing your loss. If you have access to the Internet, check out online grief support groups and Web sites.

Talk or pray to your deceased loved one—or don't talk or pray to your deceased loved one.

Go to the cemetery or don't go to the cemetery. Grieving is an individual process. For some, talking to the deceased and visiting them at the cemetery are valuable tools for accepting the finality of death. For others, these concepts do not fit well with the healing process. Whatever you choose to do, remember that it has to be right for you. Don't worry about what other people say or do.

Prepare for holidays and anniversaries.

If certain dates or times of the year are particularly difficult to deal with (especially during the first year after the death of your loved one), you may want to plan ahead. Decide if you want to commemorate the event (such as putting up a Christmas tree), celebrate it but in a different manner than previously (going out to a restaurant for dinner rather than preparing a meal at home), or plan something entirely different (taking a trip, visiting with friends, reading a book, working at a homeless shelter). Rather than letting the day sneak up on you, be ready to meet it head-on. This will go a long way in easing your pain. But do not be surprised if emotions resurface even after the second- or third-year anniversary of your loved one's death or the second or third year of celebrating certain holidays without your loved one. The grief process is long, and each curve of your journey holds an emotional change of direction. But you will be amazed at your growth. As you progress forward, each curve becomes easier to navigate, and the pain isn't quite as severe as it was at the previous bend.

If you are to heal, the journey through grief has to be *your* journey. Do what is right for you, and you will find that your journey will become a little less stressful and a little less overwhelming as time goes on. Time does heal. Time will soften your pain as you try to work through your grief; but work through it you must. You cannot ignore grief. You cannot go over it, under it, or around it. Working *through* your grief is what will bring you comfort.

WHEN YOU ARE THE ONE PROVIDING CARE

While many people will begin their journey through grief with the death of a loved one, an ever-increasing number of people actually begin months before. These people are the caregivers. The advent of hospice—as well as life-prolonging drugs, procedures, and machines—coupled with the increased cost of long-term care services, means that the seriously ill are choosing to spend their last months at home rather than in a hospital. Nursing-home care, which now averages $44,000 per year, is expected to more than quadruple by the year 2030 to over $190,600 annually. This cost will continue to be prohibitive for more and more people, who will be dependent upon their children to care for them. These children are known as the "sandwich generation" because they are forced to care for their parents as well as their own children.

For caregivers, grieving starts almost at the exact moment they begin serving in that capacity. They see the person they love beginning to slip away from them, and they experience some of the emotions associated with grief; this is known as "anticipatory grief." Caregivers may become sad, depressed, or angry; they may even resent having been put into the position of caregiver.

For the terminally ill, it is a matter of dying with dignity. But the decision to die at home changes the family dynamic by forcing certain family members into the role of caregiver. And caregivers need to be aware of several things.

The dying process may actually be worse than the death itself.

Watching a loved one suffer is extremely heart wrenching. As the disease progresses, physical and mental changes become evident. Demeanor changes. There may be less recognition of people and surroundings. These developments are all difficult for caregivers to watch. Find out about the disease so that you will be better prepared to deal with it. As difficult as it may be, try to remember that being with a loved one when that person dies is an honor and an extremely private moment. As your loved one makes the transition from life to death, you will be providing comfort.

Serving as a caregiver may be rewarding, but it is a frustrating experience.

The stress may seem unbearable.

- You will be emotionally torn between the demands of your job and family and your devotion to your terminally ill loved one.

- You must be prepared to deal with the unexpected things you cannot control, including sudden changes in the patient's condition.

- You will be physically exhausted from making medical arrangements, such as setting up a hospital bed for the home, running to the hospital or pharmacy or grocery store, keeping house, preparing meals, maintaining a schedule for medications, paying bills, and providing emotional support.

- You may be financially drained by your contribution to the medical care of the patient.

- You may have problems with other family members who do not want to assist you or who think you are trying to take over.

- You may find that worrying about so many people at one time is so stressful that you feel taken beyond the breaking point.

- You will be responsible for making the most demanding and serious decisions, including signing hospice documents, executing right to die documents, and—in all likelihood—planning the funeral.

Be aware of your own personality changes.

Because of the emotions and pressures faced by caregivers, they themselves will often go through dramatic changes in disposition. You may become difficult to deal with; you may even become nasty and mean. It is difficult to be nice all of the time—and all of your time is reserved for your dying patient. However, your relatives and true friends will understand the emotional weight you are carrying and will understand your behavior.

Know that there will be feelings of guilt.

No matter what you say or do, you will be tempted to second-guess yourself. If you take care of a parent at his or her house, you may feel guilty for not spending time with your own family. And when you are with your family, you may feel guilty for not spending time with your parent. It can be a no-win situation, but you must be aware that these feelings can occur. You need to get past those feelings. Allow for the guilt and move on.

If you are caring for a parent, you will have to face role reversal.

You may not want to take on the role of parent, but it is imperative that you do so. You will be thrust into being the overseer of your parent's life. The balance of power and responsibility will change. Try not to dwell on the role reversal and focus on the love between you and your parent.

Be careful not to make hasty decisions.

Sometimes problems regarding money and/or living arrangements will compound an already difficult situation. If you absolutely must make some decisions—such as taking a reverse home mortgage for a terminally ill parent in order to pay for professional caregivers—try to take along someone who can help you think things through and keep track of all the particulars. You may think you will be able to recall all the details, but stress will likely cause your memory to be fuzzy or mistaken.

Try to take time for yourself.

Yes, your life will be out of balance for a while, and yes, you are carrying out one of the most important tasks of your life. Most of your attention will be given to your immediate, foremost concern—your dying loved one—at the expense of all those other important people in your life. But time will heal all. Eventually the other people will come to understand. However, it is imperative that every so often you take a few minutes to unwind. Although circumstances and schedules may be hectic, read a chapter in a book or watch a favorite television show or call a friend. Just a few minutes a day will help you maintain your composure in a difficult situation.

Include your children.

Don't be afraid to give your kids the opportunity to help take care of their parent or grandparent. They may surprise you. If they are especially close to their grandparents, for instance, children may feel closer to them by helping out. In addition, the children will feel they are not only helping their grandparents but also assisting their parents. Jobs appropriate for children include getting the patient food or drink, fluffing pillows, unraveling a tangled oxygen hose, or getting a walker or wheelchair when it is needed. While children should not be forced to help, they should be given the opportunity. They will find it rewarding, and you will find it helpful.

Say good-bye.

Before medications or disease symptoms take control of the situation, you should take the opportunity to say good-bye. Even if it seems premature, telling your loved one what he or she meant to you will be a comfort to him or her and a relief to you. As your responsibilities as caregiver increase, it will become harder to find the right opportunity to express your feelings. Just tell your loved one how you have appreciated and loved him or her, how you are grateful for the time you have had together. Later, it will be consoling to know that you said what you had to say.

As a caregiver, it will be your responsibility to know when signs are pointing to the end of your loved one's life.

While there will be doctors and nurses and hospice staff available to assist you, there are certain signs that indicate that your loved one has entered into the final stages of life.

Loss of appetite and thirst. Terminal patients may go days without eating or drinking. Do not force your loved one to eat; this could be a very tiresome, very painful experience. As difficult as it may be to imagine, the terminally ill will not starve by not eating. Conversely, forcing them to eat will not prolong their life. They may experience a very dry sensation in the mouth but refuse even ice chips. Keep lip balm available, since their lips may become parched and cracked.

Changes in urinary output and bowel elimination. While one would assume that the output of urine would decrease with the diminished intake of liquid, this is not always the case; it may actually increase. In either instance, the color will probably become darker. A catheter will eliminate the urine automatically from the patient. And even though food intake may be greatly decreased, the patient's stools may increase. Both should be monitored carefully.

Confusion and diminished strength. Patients who are dying will become increasingly weaker, sleeping almost continuously twenty-four hours a day. And when they are awake, they become disoriented easily. Care should be taken to speak softly, slowly, and distinctly so as not to startle them. Your loved one may lose touch with reality, confusing conversations heard on a television or radio with those he or she thinks were with you. Keep all environmental noise to a minimum, avoiding programming such as talk shows or soaps operas, which may further confuse the patient. And always identify yourself when speaking to the terminally ill. This way they will know it is you and not have to guess who is speaking.

A sense of distance from others. It is not uncommon for the dying to start disassociating themselves from other people, even their loved ones. It will seem that he or she is ignoring you. In actuality, the patient is trying to ease into the transition from life to death, and this method is making it easier to do so. In fact, you may also notice that you yourself are establishing more distance.

Changes in breathing patterns. There will be periods during which your loved one does not breathe at all. This is known as apnea. While it is frightening to those around the patient, this is not painful to the patient and is common, even among healthy people. As your loved one gets closer to the end, the jaw muscles will relax more and more and the patient will be breathing almost exclusively through the mouth. Eventually, secretions may back up into the windpipe. As he or she continues to breathe, these secretions will make a gurgling sound—what is commonly referred to as the death rattle.

Restlessness. Near the very end, your loved one may become fidgety or extremely restless. He or she may have conversations with people who have died or who are not present in the room. Hearing someone talk like this may be very disconcerting. But it is a part of the dying process that many people experience.

The ability to hear what's going on in the room. Almost right up to the end, the dying person will most likely be able to hear you and other people in the room. Take care what you say while in the room. You can comfort a dying person by praying softly, playing soft background music, holding the person's hand, and simply having soothing conversation. These activities help the dying know that they are in the company of people who love them.

If you feel that your loved one is fighting against the end of life, whisper that it is OK to let go. That may be what the person has been waiting to hear. Finally, if you have not already said good-bye, these last moments may offer a chance for a private farewell. You know what thoughts are in your mind and what feelings are in your heart—force them out! You may fumble for the words or start to cry, but what matters most is that you say good-bye. You will always treasure your last words with your loved one. Not only will you have comforted your loved one during those final steps from life to death, but you will have taken one of the first steps toward recovery on your own journey through grief.

WHEN YOU ARE THE ONE WHO MUST BREAK THE NEWS

Telling another person that someone has died is never an easy task. For some, it may be the most difficult job they have ever been given. However, some simple guidelines can make it a little easier.

Be as gentle as possible.

It makes no difference whether you are the person who was with the deceased when he or she died or the person who has to track down survivors and break the sad news. You were given the task, and you must follow through with it. Even if you feel uncomfortable making the phone call, the family has entrusted you with this task. Just remember to soften the blow as best you can. Be as calm and tearless as possible.

If you need to give instructions, do it before you break the bad news.

For instance: "You need to go to the ATM, withdraw $100, and take a cab to your mother's. She asked me to get hold of you to tell you that your dad passed away this morning. You need to get there as soon as you can." Be prepared to repeat the information several times and to offer as much assistance as you can. Perhaps you can offer to pick up people and drive them where they need to be.

Be as straightforward as you can when breaking bad news to children.

For instance: "I've got some bad news about Grandma. She got very sick during the night, and she couldn't get better, and I'm afraid she died." Be prepared to answer any questions, but don't load children with too much information. Just make sure that they know they can come to you at any time with questions about the death of their loved one. And take care to reassure children that the death was in no way their fault. Sometimes children think that their own bad actions, words, or even secret thoughts are somehow connected to a death.

Be cordial and to the point when making calls to friends and relatives of the deceased.

Be as informative as possible: "Is this the McGuire residence? My name is Robert, and I'm calling on behalf of your cousin John. He asked me to call and tell you that his wife passed away last night. I have the information for you regarding the wake and funeral." Be prepared to answer questions such as "How did it happen?" "How are John and the kids doing?" "Is there anything I can do?" "Was John with her when she died?" "Where exactly is the funeral home located?" While you may not know all the answers, give whatever information you believe the bereaved wants made known, particularly if there are any questions concerning the nature of the death.

Use the address book and/or Christmas card list of both the deceased and the family for whom you are making notification calls.

It is too easy to forget to call someone. Or you may not even be aware of certain friends of the deceased who should be told. If you make a call and can't get through, write the name down and try again later. Don't rely on remembering to call a person again later. And if you must leave a message on an answering machine, don't blurt out everything on the machine. Say something like: "This is Betty Roberts. I have some very urgent news about Bill, which I must share with you. It is very important that you call me as soon as possible. I can be reached at . . ." If you know you will be away from the telephone for a period of time and will be unable to answer return calls, do leave as complete a message as you can. Just be as gentle as possible: "This is Tom Johnston. I am calling with some sad news about Jean. I'm afraid that she passed away last night at about 9:00."

HOW TO HELP IMMEDIATELY AFTER SOMEONE HAS DIED

At the time of the death:

- Visit the family.
- If appropriate, offer to help the family make funeral arrangements.
- Make phone calls to friends and relatives.
- Let out-of-town people stay at your home or offer to drive them to or from the airport, bus, or train station.
- Drive people to or from the funeral home.
- Take care of indoor plants; cut or water lawns.

- Help with the smaller children. Read them a story, help with homework, offer to take them on an outing or care for them during the funeral service.

- Prepare meals, do laundry, run errands, clean house, buy groceries, or house-sit during the wake and/or funeral.

- Assist with the planning of the funeral service and offer to participate.

- Help with the funeral luncheon.

- If the bereaved is on medications, find out which ones and when they should be taken. Remind the bereaved to take them during this stressful time.

- Offer to take care of pets or take them to the kennel for boarding.

- Take in newspapers and mail.

- Attend the wake or funeral and allow yourself to cry with the bereaved.

After the funeral:

- Help with acknowledgments, correspondence, and messages. Although this task helps the bereaved work through the reality of the death, you can offer to address or put stamps on envelopes. *Do not take over this entire project!* Grievers may not understand at the time, but *they* need to complete this job.

- Offer to help the mourners remove personal effects, when they are ready to do so. Don't decide for them which items to give away, but help pack boxes, fold clothes, and so forth.

- Listen to the requests mourners make regarding the disposition of personal effects. For example, clothes may be sent to charities, and residual craft materials may be sent to senior citizen homes to be used by others.

- Invite the bereaved out for shopping, dinner, a movie, a drive, or a trip to the cemetery. Extend these invitations repeatedly, even if they have been refused in the past. It is important for them to hear your concern for them, and it reassures them that they have not been forgotten.

- Offer to help the grievers organize bills, balance checking accounts, or discuss insurance issues. Although funeral directors are now frequently assisting families in these matters, the bereaved may feel more comfortable having help from someone close to them.

- Bring over casseroles or other meals, go grocery shopping, mow the lawn, shovel snow, take out the garbage, or baby-sit.

- On the six-month and twelve-month anniversaries of the death, call, visit, or send a note or card to let the bereaved know that you are remembering them and the departed. Do the same on the deceased's birthday and wedding anniversary. Be sure to mention the deceased by name.

- Remember the bereaved during all holidays that first year. These will be particularly difficult times. Offer assistance but understand that each person copes with events differently. Many will want to skip the holiday entirely. Take the lead from them.

HOW TO DEAL WITH FUNERAL ARRANGEMENTS

Once a loved one has died—whether the death was unexpected or anticipated—you move painfully into what can be referred to as "impact grief." It is overwhelming to realize that your loved one will be with you no longer and that the death will have life-altering effects on you and your family. You become aware of the immediate situation's urgency, of the decisions that need to be made in the next few days. Panic may set in. You might feel as if you are on a collision course with no indication as to where or when you will crash. But this is just the beginning point in your journey through grief; you will not yet have begun to miss the deceased in quite the same way that you will in the coming weeks, months, and maybe even years, as the actual grieving process sets in.

One of the first tasks you will have to face while you are experiencing impact grief is deciding what will happen to the body of your loved one over the next several days.

Arrange to have the body taken to a funeral home or crematorium.

Many families have neighborhood undertakers or funeral homes that were used by other family members, friends, or neighbors. But if you do not have a funeral home already in mind, you will have to choose one. The Federal Trade Commission mandates that funeral homes keep a list of prices for their services, making comparison shopping possible. These prices may or may not include the price of the casket. If you choose, you may purchase a casket from a casket store. These stores are a relatively new concept and will usually provide caskets at a reasonably low price. Whichever you choose, you must know your budget. Usually the amount you spend is dictated by the amount of insurance held by the deceased. Should your budget be flexible, it is still advisable to stay within your means. There may be unanticipated expenses that you will have to deal with later. Extremely nice and comforting services are possible without extravagant costs.

Call the chosen funeral home or the appropriate authorities.

If the deceased died in a hospital, the staff will arrange with the funeral home for the body to be removed. If your loved one died at home, and it was an expected death—assisted by a hospice agency, for instance—a call to the funeral home is all that is needed to arrange for the removal of the body. If, however, the person who died lived alone and/or the death was unexpected—during sleep, for instance—the authorities will probably have to be notified. Depending upon the individual's state of residence, there is a reasonable chance that the body will have to be taken to a hospital for the pronouncement of death.

In this case, the death certificate will most likely list the hospital, not the home, as the place of death. If the death is mysterious or if there is a desire not to have the body taken to a hospital, a call will have to be made to the county coroner. The coroner might take the body to the coroner's office for an autopsy.

Be prepared to make certain decisions before meeting with the funeral director to make final arrangements.

Make sure everyone has been notified—that is, every member of the immediate family and anyone who is to be included in making the funeral arrangements (see page 20, "When You Are the One Who Must Break the News").

Decide whether you want an actual wake and funeral or whether you would rather just have a memorial service at a later date. Another option that's becoming increasingly popular is to have a brief wake—one or two hours—followed immediately by a memorial service and then the cemetery service, all in one day. A third option is cremation, with no wake at all.

Choose the clothes in which to have your loved one buried. This can be extremely difficult, especially if you never discussed this or if the deceased has lost substantial weight. Your options include bringing clothes previously worn by the deceased (these can be made to fit), buying new clothes, or choosing clothes at the funeral home.

Regarding the services, make a list of the details that are most important to you. Which church, if any, will be used for the final services? If jewelry will be on the deceased during the wake, do you want it removed before the final closing? You can present this list to the funeral director. Do not rely on your memory. The emotions of the moment will diminish your ability to remember.

Decide which family members will participate in the services and in what capacity. If there is to be a photo collage for the wake, who will put it together? Can you have—and do you want—a video or slide presentation at the chapel? Who will serve as pallbearers? Will there be testimonials or eulogies at the Mass or memorial service? If so, who will deliver them? Will there be readers? If the service will be a Catholic mass, who will bring up the gifts? What about music? Are there certain songs you want played or sung?

If you have not already done so, you will have to choose a cemetery for the burial. You may have to decide if other family members will be buried in adjoining lots. While the funeral director can help you with this, and even take you to the cemetery to purchase lots, you may want to decide ahead of time which cemetery will be the final resting place for your loved one. If the remains of your loved one are to be cremated, you will have to decide what will happen to the ashes. Will you dispose of them by having the urn placed in a mausoleum or will you have the ashes scattered?

Consider having the music and eulogies recorded for play-back at a later time. Although this is not a normal request, many times mourners are in shock and will not be able to recall the music or spoken words that were so comforting at the funeral. If the funeral director cannot accommodate you, ask a friend to make the recording for you. You might also ask the priest or minister for a typed copy of the eulogy. Not only will out-of-town relatives and friends who are unable to attend appreciate receiving this, it will also be a fond remembrance for you.

Consider making the funeral service available over the Internet. Though a relatively new concept and not yet available everywhere, funeral web-casting is seen as a viable alternative for people unable to attend a funeral in person. The services can be broadcast live or recorded and can be made password accessible only, if the family so requests. People around the world can view the funeral in real time. This option offers the additional means of pre-serving the services on CD for viewing at a later date.

Find out whether or not the funeral home has facilities for serving food and decide whether you want to avail yourself of this accommodation. Will your family be sharing com-mon areas with other families for other wakes? Can the funeral home keep them separate? Do you bring in sand-wiches and pastries or have a caterer bring in something more substantial? Do you run home for a bite to eat or stop at a restaurant? It is important to keep up strength, so eating is a must. Keep in mind that whenever you leave a wake, even for a short time, there's the risk that you will miss seeing someone who comes by to offer condolences.

Decide whether you want a luncheon to follow the funeral services. This is an added cost that you may wish to avoid. But if you decide to have one, consideration must be made for family traditions. Does your family have sandwiches and sweets back at the house? Do family members, friends, and neighbors chip in for a "potluck" buffet? Maybe the local church will offer its facilities for a luncheon. Is there a family restaurant that is a particular favorite? If not, decide where the luncheon will be held and what you want served. Will there be one entree or a choice of meals? Will drinks be served? Will guests be invited by a general announcement by the funeral director at the conclusion of the services, or will guests be asked to attend by special invitation?

The funeral director will be your point of contact for the next several days.

All arrangements regarding the days, times, and place of services will be made through him or her. Some of the items the funeral director will be assisting you with include the following:

A burial vault for the cemetery. Be aware that at certain cemeteries you can purchase burial lots at a price that includes the vault and the headstone.

Special features to the service if the deceased was a veteran. The funeral director can help arrange for a flag for the casket, honor guard, military salute, and so forth.

Death notices or obituaries. The funeral director can prepare and place the death notice or obituary, neither of which has to be the standard "copy only" variety. Death notices are often listed alphabetically in your newspapers; they usually list the survivors and the particulars of the wake and funeral. Obituaries generally chronicle the life of the deceased and will list survivors but no wake details. Ordinarily there is a cost associated with each, although some smaller local papers may publish them for free. Pictures may now be included with death notices. Also, there are Web sites that will list the obituary and information about the funeral home, directions for getting there, and so forth. If you want to use a Web site, ask the funeral director to assist you.

Items for the wake and funeral. The funeral director will arrange for limousines, flowers, guest book, remembrance cards, and other details. If you are requesting roses for display at the wake and you want to have them saved for use after the funeral, tell the funeral director. You can have the flowers sent to a nursing home or have remembrances made out of them, such as pendants, tie tacs, and rosaries. And, while it has become increasingly popular to include the phrase "no flowers" in obituaries, consider allowing other mourners to send floral arrangements to the funeral home. It is a sign of respect to the deceased and a show of affection to the survivors. This was clearly demonstrated at the deaths of Princess Diana and John F. Kennedy, Jr, when thousands of people left or sent flowers as expressions of grief and sympathy. People need and want to express their feelings, and giving flowers does just that. Some may think it's wasteful, but to others it's a thoughtful gesture.

Luncheon arrangements. On the day of the funeral, the director will notify the restaurant or caterers the number of people who will be present for the luncheon.

Death certificate and other official matters. After the funeral, the funeral director will arrange for copies of the death certificate. This document serves as the official record that your loved one is deceased. It will be required for numerous transactions including processing your claims for insurance, IRA, and Social Security death benefits as well as changing the name on your home or car title, on your checking, savings, and trust accounts, and on your stocks and bonds. Be sure to estimate high the number of certificates you require. It will be easier, faster, and cheaper to request death certificates now than at a later time. The funeral director will also handle insurance and social security issues and the headstone placement.

At this stressful time, try to remember that your wishes are the top priority.

You have a definite say-so as to all arrangements. Do not be afraid to assert yourself. Your requests should be honored unless what you're asking for is against the law or physically impossible. Do not let others—including funeral directors or clergy—intimidate you. If, for instance, a funeral director suggests that placing flower petals on the casket at the cemetery will ruin the casket and shouldn't be done, don't be discouraged. Try to compromise: perhaps the flowers could be placed on the casket at the end of the service but removed prior to the burial.

Be aware of people in the funeral industry who may try to take advantage of your situation.

You may want to take along a friend whose judgment is not clouded by grief. While most funeral directors will be considerate, honest, and sensitive to your needs, a rare few will try to talk you into unnecessary expenses. Here are some problems to watch out for:

Preparing the body. If you are cremating your loved one, you probably will not need to have the body embalmed, nor will you need a casket—you certainly won't need an expensive one. If in doubt, check with other funeral directors in your area.

Buying a casket. Do not be coerced into purchasing a casket way above your means. Some undertakers may play upon your emotions by telling you how important it is to honor the memory of your loved one by purchasing an expensive casket. A less expensive casket will fulfill the same function as one costing thousands of dollars. In fact, caskets that are presented as "waterproof and airtight" may actually cause the body to decay at a faster pace, due to a buildup of gases.

Service charges. If you purchase your casket somewhere other than the funeral home, make sure the funeral home does not add a service charge. The Federal Trade Commission prohibits such a charge.

Signing the contract. Before you sign a contract, make sure the funeral director provides you with an itemized price list.

After the funeral, attend first to those responsibilities that actually pertain to the wake and funeral.

Send thank-you cards and letters; arrange for memorials in the name of the deceased; make notes about the sermon or eulogy or music while they are fresh in your memory. Provide the funeral director with any documents he or she might need to help arrange for payment by the insurance company. Remember to save all envelopes for cards, memorials, masses, etc. received at home until you have sent all the thank-you notes. Mistakes do happen, and sometimes the wrong name will be listed on a notification card. Keeping the envelope might help you find out who actually sent it.

WHAT TO DO TO SUPPORT THOSE WHO ARE GRIEVING

Do listen.

Be there for them, even if their grief is prolonged (which may last years instead of weeks, as many mistakenly expect). Surround them with as much comfort, love, and understanding as possible, but remember to give them some private time as well. Be there for them, but remember to give them space.

Do validate their feelings.

Acknowledge and support them. Even if what they are expressing seems strange or is frustrating to you, it may be very real to them. Often they need to hear aloud what they are thinking in their heads. They will have to tell their story.

Do allow them to tell and retell the story.

They may need to repeat and recount—and repeat and recount again—stating every detail of how the loved one died. Be a good listener. Allow the bereaved the opportunity to tell the story again and again, and most important, do not try to "fix" their pain by relating stories of your own. To do so only diminishes their grief. It doesn't take away their pain but actually prolongs it. They must be allowed to experience their own ups and downs. Reiteration of the details of the death is an important first step of the healing process.

Do remember important anniversaries and holidays.

Sending a card or note or making a call on the deceased's birthday, date of death, or wedding anniversary is appropriate and appreciated even for years afterward. The grievers will be glad to know that the loved one is remembered by others.

Do mention the deceased by name.

Those in mourning notice when the deceased is no longer referred to by his or her name. To those who are grieving, this translates into, "He doesn't matter to anyone, anymore.

Everyone has forgotten him. No one cares." In addition, grievers may believe that their own lives have no value and that they are no longer important.

Do be aware of, and prepared for, the emotions the grievers may be experiencing.

Anger, anguish, anxiety, confusion, denial, depression, despair, disbelief, emptiness, guilt, heartache, helplessness, loneliness, numbness, regret, resentment, shock, sorrow, and tearfulness are all possible responses to grief. The bereaved may become stressed, physically ill, worried about money, and unable to sleep (or sluggish and likely to sleep more than usual). They may feel left out, be unable to communicate with friends or relatives, or be unable to leave the house. At other times, they may talk incessantly or be unable to stay in the house one more minute. The passing of time may generate additional feelings of letting go, of needing to deal with unfinished business, or of losing one's identity. Sound overwhelming? It is. That's why grievers need support.

Do talk to grievers.

Be sure to use positive phrases, such as:

- "I'm so sorry about your loss."
- "Please accept our deepest sympathies."
- "This must be a very difficult time for you and your family. How are you coping?"
- "I don't know what I can say, but I want you to know how very sorry I am and that I care."

- "Do you feel like talking?"

- "I've been thinking about you and wanted to see how you've been doing."

Or, as a ten year old proclaimed, "Just go up to them and say 'I love you.'"

If you are uncomfortable talking with the bereaved at the wake or funeral, it is OK to just stand in silence with them. However, if you are feeling awkward, don't just walk away. Tell the grievers that you realize there are other people they must talk to and that you will be sitting in the back of the chapel, if they feel like talking later. Or tactfully switch to a thoughtful gesture, such as:

- "Let me get you a glass of water."

- "Why don't I get you a tissue?"

- "I'll get you a sweater."

People in grief need your support. But it is imperative to understand the importance of saying the right words. If ever you feel compelled to say something like "Stop your crying; pretty soon you'll be getting on with your life" or any words to that effect, reread this section.

Do consider touching the griever.

A gentle pat, an extra firm handshake, a grasping of the hand or arm, or an embrace—all are messages of reassurance, caring, compassion, sorrow, and strength. You have no idea how far a hug or any extra kindness during the wake or funeral can go to comfort the bereaved. Long after the loved one is buried, the bereaved will remember who gave them a hug during the wake or funeral. Often, words are unnecessary. If, however, you know that a particular mourner does not like to be touched, comforting words from the heart will suffice.

Do remember that at the death of a child, the grandparents should be remembered as well as the parents and siblings.

The grandparents will be grieving not only for their lost grandchild but also for their own child. Parents hate to see their child going through such a terrible and sad experience and will actually be grieving twice. Be sure to offer your condolences to them as you would to other family members. Even if you are just acquaintances of the grandparents, they will cherish the fact that you went out of your way to pay your respects to them.

Do go up to a child and offer your condolences to him or her on the loss of a loved one.

A simple "I'm sorry your grandpa died" will make a lasting impression and will bring comfort to that child. Quite often children are totally forgotten at wakes and memorial services. If you are attending a wake where you know children will be present, make them a priority of yours. Bring along coloring books and crayons or perhaps a little puzzle to help keep them occupied. Have them show you the lounge, where they can assist you in getting something to eat or drink. Or make them feel important by giving them some little job to do, such as passing out the remembrance cards as people leave, counting the floral pieces, placing sympathy and Mass cards on the designated stand.

The children will remember your kindness, and the parents will appreciate your thoughtfulness.

Do offer your help to those who are caring for a terminally ill person.

Dealing with an anticipated death is very stressful. Offer to sit with their loved one for a few hours to give them a break. Send a little note or "Thinking of You" card to the caregivers, offering them moral support and letting them know that you are thinking of them during a difficult time. Or, offer to do something that they are unable to do because of the situation: go over to their house and cut the grass; make some meals that can be frozen and prepared whenever it is convenient for them; offer to go grocery shopping or do other chores to make things easier. Any act of kindness you perform will be remembered and treasured.

WHAT NOT TO DO TO SUPPORT THOSE WHO ARE GRIEVING

Don't judge grievers.

It is impossible to understand fully what grievers are going through. To correct them constantly or to express your viewpoints on personal matters may give the impression that you know what is best for them. And that is not possible! Should you offer comments or suggestions, be sure that you avoid condescension.

Don't inadvertently manipulate grievers.

Be available, but don't try to take over for them. Grievers need and want to be involved with the activities and responsibilities that come with mourning—but at their own pace. Respect that. Don't feel that you have to fix everything.

Don't give the grievers any of your personal medications or remedies.

They may be on medication already. And, at this vulnerable time especially, any medications must be overseen by a physician. Sedatives and other drugs are more likely to hinder grief than help it.

Don't say things that may be offensive to adult grievers.

These include the following:

- "I know just how you feel."
- "Get a grip on yourself. I never thought you'd take it this hard."
- "This isn't the time to fall apart."
- "You've got to be strong for the kids."
- "Calm down, it'll be all right."
- "Now, now, no tears!"
- "Why do you keep going over and over everything? You're only making it worse."
- "Why didn't you call me?"
- "It's a blessing in disguise."
- "I never did trust that particular hospital [or doctor, or whatever]."

- "You're young. You'll marry again."
- "You must get on with your life."
- "I know what you're going through."
- "You're so lucky to have had her for so many years. My mom died at such a young age."
- "You must be relieved that this whole ordeal is over. It's been such a strain on you."

After the death of an unborn or newly born child:

- "It's better this way."
- "At least you didn't really know the child."
- "Who knows, maybe the child was retarded or would have been sickly."

Don't say things that may be offensive to kids in grief.

- "God loved your daddy so much that he took him to heaven."
- "Be strong. Now you must help run the family."

Don't talk to the griever just for the sake of talking.

Attempts to fill the gaps of silence often lead to inappropriate comments. Just be a good listener. The bereaved will know that your taking the time from your busy schedule is an indication of your concern and your affection and is a true act of kindness.

WHEN YOU ARE A "GRIEF MANAGER"

A grief manager is a close friend or relative who assists mourners by protecting them from the unnecessary details of a death, especially a "sensational" one. He or she is responsible for lessening the bewilderment of a murder, a suicide, or the unexpected but gruesome death of a loved one. In a death that attracts worldwide attention, someone handles the media by acting as a spokesperson. After the tragic death of John F. Kennedy, Jr, a Kennedy cousin answered questions and read statements to the media. To protect relatives and friends who are not used to handling the barrage of questions from reporters, someone is appointed to that task. In addition, he or she—perhaps a son-in-law or a neighbor—may even make funeral arrangements with the funeral home and/or church, sparing the bereaved from having to deal with the media face-to-face.

The grief manager's tasks are varied.

He or she may act as the spokesperson when any media attention is brought upon the family in light of the death. The task of the grief manager may simply involve helping to make funeral arrangements for a person who has died a natural and expected death. In either instance, the grief manager has been given primary responsibility for handling arrangements and shielding mourners from aspects of the funeral with which they do not want to deal. For instance, a surviving spouse who struggles with a serious illness or handicap may appoint someone else to do what he or she would do if able.

Because the grief manager is so involved in managing the grief of others, he or she may not be able to manage his or her own grief.

Often the grief manager for a family is the husband and father, who is extremely close to the deceased. Since he also may be acting as a "buffer" between his family and the death situation, he may believe that he has to spare his family's feelings or lessen the grief experience for them. He may cover up disturbing facts about the death, make all the funeral arrangements, screen phone calls, and coordinate visits from friends. His feelings may be buried under the weight of the responsibility he has shouldered.

The grief manager must not shield the mourners more than is expected or desired.

Holding back too much information from family members is not advisable. If, for instance, details of a death were particularly frightful and the grief manager does not tell the bereaved, there is a good chance they will find out anyway. Well-meaning people at the wake will almost surely make a statement referring to this issue and leave the family bewildered. It is always good to err on the side of caution; therefore, provide small details at first. Expand upon them as the family absorbs what you have already told them. Provide additional details only if the family desires them.

Understanding Different Kinds of Grief

There is no grief which time does not lessen and soften.

Cicero, Epistolae, *IV.v*

PEOPLE GRIEVE differently depending upon the circumstances. Grieving the loss of a spouse (or life partner) is generally considered to be the most stressful event a person can encounter during a lifetime. Changes in living arrangements, social engagements, child rearing, retirement plans, and even financial security can result from the loss of a person's significant other. The loss of a parent or sibling, while devastating, may bring a whole different set of changes to tackle. Each type of grief is unique, as is each person's reaction to that grief. But each must be dealt with in order for the bereaved to find healing.

WHEN YOUR SPOUSE OR PARTNER HAS DIED

The death of a spouse or partner—regardless of whether or not children are involved—is the most stressful event you will encounter in your lifetime. You will feel lost and abandoned, and the loneliness will be severe, regardless of family size. (See chapter 4 for issues regarding children and grief.)

Accept the severity of your loss.

The loss of your spouse means the loss of your future life together. Regardless of how long you were married or living together, the length of the relationship is irrelevant in terms of the grieving process. Whether you were together five months, five years, or fifty years, you will still feel cheated, and you will still grieve. Whether it was planning a family together, raising children together, or enjoying retirement together, many options cease to exist. You have lost your soul mate. For those couples who were not rewarded with children or who chose not to have kids, life together is gone. The newly married and those who had not yet started their family are robbed of their dreams of having children together and bringing up a family. For those couples with children, family events such as graduations and vacations will be forever marked by the absence of the deceased parent. There is only one parent left to raise the children and watch them grow. Even those couples in or nearing retirement are robbed of future plans together, such as traveling and visiting the grand-children. Because of this, you, as the surviving spouse, may feel anger, frustration, or hate. Understand that these are normal feelings at this time; you are not a horrible person for possessing these emotions.

If you must learn new duties, do so slowly.

Learning to pay bills or to use the washing machine can be difficult, especially when you are in a fragile emotional state. Don't be afraid to ask for help. Family and friends will be glad to provide assistance, provided they know that you want it. And don't overlook the help that professionals can give. If balancing a checkbook is now your responsibility, don't hesitate to call your bank for help. Even the simplest tasks—pumping your own gas or shoveling snow—may seem like an enormous chore. Don't be afraid to ask for help. For example, while one widow may want to keep her husband's voice as the greeting on an answering machine, another may find it painful to hear her husband's voice. If you prefer, for safety's sake, to keep a male voice on your machine, enlist the aid of a male friend to record a new message for you. People care and will be there for you; they will not think less of you if you choose to do what you are comfortable doing. If, for instance, you decide to leave your husband's name on return mailing labels, your friends and family will support you.

Review your financial situation.

Update any documents that need to be changed: checking and savings accounts, stock certificates, mortgage, car titles, car insurance, charge accounts, and certificates for jointly owned property. You may find that you have no credit history because all the bills and home utilities were in your spouse's name, not yours. You may be denied credit for this reason. Don't hesitate to get help from friends or even professional financial advisors. Ask people you know for the names of financial advisors who have good reputations. You may need their help only for a short while, but for now you need support as you deal with financial realities.

Find the best way to get good sleep.

Sleeping alone may be very disturbing for you. If it is difficult to sleep now that you're alone, consider moving to your spouse's bed or your spouse's side of the bed. Comedian George Burns, who had trouble sleeping after the death of his wife, Gracie Allen, finally found slumber when he started sleeping where Gracie used to sleep. You may find that doing so may actually make you feel closer to the deceased than before. If this doesn't work, try moving to another bedroom or another room entirely; try sleeping on the couch in the family room. Some people find it helpful to put a pillow behind their backs to provide the sensation of the spouse or partner in the bed.

Deal with feelings of loneliness.

If you are afraid to be alone, keeping the radio or television constantly on may be helpful. If coming home to an empty house is painful, try arranging your time so that you will arrive while it is still light outside. Or buy timers that automatically turn on lights before you return home. Do not feel that you need to answer to others. Do what is best for you.

Take your time in deciding how you will dispose of your spouse's belongings.

Know that certain items may serve as catalysts in reviving fond memories, which may lead to tears. These items must be dealt with, but they don't have to be removed immediately. Some people will want them gone right away due to the pain they cause. But if you aren't sure what to do with a loved one's possessions, don't do anything yet. It might be that you will want to donate some items to charity; other things you might want to give to certain family members as a remembrance of your loved one. Whatever you decide, taking your time to make the decisions is usually the wisest thing to do. It is not uncommon for years to pass before the survivor completes this task.

If you make arrangements with someone to assist you in some way—helping you grocery shop, for instance—be sure to do something nice in return.

Repayment for a kind deed is usually not expected or necessary. But how nice it is—even months later—to give an unexpected gift as a special sign of your appreciation. Of course, repayment does not necessarily mean payment by money—you could baby-sit, invite the person to dinner, or fill up his or her car with gasoline. Whatever you choose will be appreciated.

Be aware of the "fifth-wheel" syndrome in social situations.

Initial experiences of being alone at social gatherings can be difficult. Prepare yourself up front for the emotions that may overcome you. People may seem distant because they are a "couple" and you are a "single." Some people may actually view you as a threat to their own relationships, because now you are single again. Longtime friends might suddenly drop out of sight; this is especially likely if these people were actually your spouse's friends before they were your friends. Perhaps your spouse was the one who generated the most energy in your social network, and so now you feel adrift and unable to keep up former relationships. You might find that, in addition to the loss of your spouse, you will suffer the loss of friends as well.

Don't avoid dealing with your sexual feelings.

You may miss having someone for a companion, and you may miss the sexual aspects of your marriage. Be aware of these feelings and work through them however is best for you. Do not be embarrassed to discuss this with a doctor, with clergy, or with a close friend. But do not simply ignore these feelings; they may not simply disappear. If they persist and you are unable to resolve them, consider seeing a counselor or psychiatrist for assistance.

Try not to be too critical or moody.

If your demeanor is constantly negative, you may drive away friends and family. Work on this as best you can. The disbelief that your partner is gone may last a very long time, but your outward behavior does not need to reflect this. Also, be aware of your own reactions to circumstances. For example, are you laughing at a sad story—a response that is unusual for you and would normally be regarded as inappropriate? This may be an indication that you are denying the death of your spouse.

Work on your own grief.

While you are busy helping your children work through their grief, you may find that you are falling into a pattern of *not* working on your own grief and feelings. Because you—by yourself—have to deal with the kids and their changing emotions and outbursts, your feelings may be put on the back burner. You are caring for the kids, you've had to go back to work, and there may be no time for you to grieve. You may be frustrated and think, *When will it be my turn to grieve? When is it my turn to take care of me?* This is an understandable reaction, and it must be dealt with. If you or one of your children has a difficult time healing, seek professional support. Grieving is a natural process, but sometimes we don't understand how to let it happen. And other stresses and responsibilities can easily get in the way of processing grief.

WHEN YOUR PARENT HAS DIED

The death of a parent is often the most underestimated in terms of impact—especially to adult sons and daughters—yet it is the most common form of bereavement. Some people may not have spouses; others may not have siblings or children. But parents are common to each and every one of us. The death of a parent means the loss of someone we have known and probably respected all our lives.

The death of an older parent or a parent who was seriously ill may not be perceived as a significant loss.

People will constantly remind you that he or she "lived a full life" or "it was his time to go" or "you're lucky to have had her as long as you did." These statements tend to minimize your loss. The fact remains that this is a loss of great proportions. Do not let the misguided statements of others wrongly steer you into believing that you shouldn't be grieving at all or that you should be grieving only a short while. A loss is a loss, and the loss of a parent is major. You will need to journey through grief, at your own pace and in your own manner.

Adult children who were close to their parents will miss not only their parents but also the regular contact they had with them.

You will feel that now there is no one to tell your troubles to or go to for advice. You may feel that you have lost your protector, someone you could turn to in times of trouble. Many adult children pay regular visits to their parents and go to certain events with them. Thus, you may be mourning the loss of a friend as well as a parent.

You may have the feeling that you are closer to death.

This is a very real and normal reaction and can be expected after a parent dies. After all, your childhood belief that your parents are immortal has been shattered. Even adults have the feeling that parents are somehow less vulnerable to death than other people. Once you lose a parent to death, it's a logical next step to feel that you, yourself, are more likely to die soon.

The death of your second parent means additional adjustments.

Besides carrying the burden of grief, you now become the "next generation," the matriarch or patriarch of the family. You become, in essence, the keeper of the family tree; you are responsible for passing on the family history to future generations. But with the death of your second parent, you lose access to both parents' remembrances, their fond memories of events that occurred before you were born. Another significant aspect of losing the second parent is that there is no parent left with which to grieve this new loss.

You can't go home again.

Your childhood home—which may have been your home all your life—and all the possessions within the house may now be gone. If it is sold, you may never be able to go there again. You will realize, over and over again, that you no longer have that home to go home to. In all likelihood, you may feel like you are an orphan no matter what your age. You have no parents, no home, and you feel very alone. You are no one's child. These are all very normal reactions to the loss of parents. You will not be the first person to feel like this, and you won't be the last. It is a part of the grieving process that many adult children will experience and will need to work out. Even if the dwelling your parent was living in was not a childhood home but an apartment or a condo that you never lived in, you will still feel a sense of abandonment. There still is no place to go where you can see and visit your parents.

WHEN YOUR CHILD HAS DIED

When a parent dies, you lose your past; but when a child dies, you lose your future. Hopes, dreams, and the loving closeness of a family are shattered. The loss of a child tears at the heart like nothing else; it's the world gone crazy. Parents aren't supposed to bury children—it's against every law of nature. But parents bury children every day. And when your child dies, a huge part of you dies too, leaving you brokenhearted, depressed, and overwhelmed.

Parents who are dealing with the death of a child or children will often experience additional physiological effects and emotional symptoms.

Facial expressions may change, voices may begin to shake during conversations, sleep may be disrupted, memory may deteriorate, concentration may drop off, self-confidence may diminish. Parents may feel that because their child is dead, it must be their fault, regardless of the situation or circumstances. Talking about anything—even if it's just about the different ways the two of you are grieving—will be a first step in communicating with and helping each other.

Because everyone grieves differently, lack of communication between spouses may cause them to distance themselves from each other.

While the strengths of each partner may surface at this time, differences will remain. One partner may want to talk about the death while the other doesn't; one may cry all the time and the other not at all. One person may want to be intimate to rekindle the sense of closeness lost by the death of the child; his or her spouse may find such a thought repugnant. Divorce becomes a real possibility for couples who lose a child. Guard against alienating yourself from your spouse. If differences remain, the assistance of a counselor or support group is highly recommended.

The grief of the parents may be so overwhelming that they don't realize to what extent their surviving children are suffering.

These brave children may feel that they are being deprived of attention because their parents are too busy grieving the deceased sibling. Surviving children may think that their parents would rather another of their children had died instead. You must talk with your children and comfort them. Tell them how sad you are that their brother or sister has died but how happy you are that they are here with you. Explain that no parents ever want any of their children to die. Ask them to help you think of ways the family can grieve together and how they can honor their brother or sister. Give each surviving child a special memento of the deceased child. Finally, be watchful of any changes in your children's behavior. This is a highly stressful time for them, and they may seek relief from their feelings through any number of outlets, including substance abuse or "acting out."

One or both parents may stay in denial for a prolonged period of time.

To avoid facing the reality of your child's death, you may spend a lot of time and energy on funeral arrangements while neglecting to stand at the casket and grieve your loss. Later, this avoidance may translate into workaholism. Yes, it hurts every time you think of your child being dead. But you must face this pain and learn to deal with it. It is unhealthy to avoid the topic or delay your grieving. Meet it now. There are no shortcuts along the journey through grief, and if you delay the beginning, you only prolong—not shorten—the journey itself.

A child's possessions do not need to be removed right away.

Don't worry about cleaning out your child's room immediately. There is no need to rush into this job; it should not be one of your highest priorities. Your energy and your focus will be spent on emotions and other reactions to your loss. To worry about removing your child's belongings will only add to the load. It may be that you want to see the child's belongings one more time. Perhaps sitting in the child's room will make you feel closer to him or her. You will know when the time is right to deal with the child's possessions.

Well into the grieving process, parents may feel guilty for experiencing enjoyment again.

You will probably fear that you're being a bad parent if you laugh or have fun. You may feel disloyal to the memory of your deceased child. Yet it is not only permissible but also healthy to live again. Life must go on, and in as normal a manner as possible. However, be sure that you are moving on with your life because you have moved through your grieving and not because you have avoided grieving.

The loss of an adult child brings additional issues.

Well-meaning but uninformed people may not see the death of an adult child in the same way they see the death of a baby or adolescent. They may think that the pain is somehow not as great. You will know better. Others will probably remind you that you were "lucky to have had him as long as you did"; if it was a sudden death, you will be told how lucky she was not to have suffered. Parents of a deceased married child may have to take a back seat to the spouse's and grandchildren's grief. There may not be an immediate outlet to express your own grief. You may be expected to watch the grandchildren and to set an example for them. Still, it is important that you somehow make time to express your own sadness and emotions.

WHEN YOUR UNBORN OR
NEWLY BORN CHILD HAS DIED

Suggestions already mentioned in the previous section apply to this situation as well. However, we have given this category of loss a separate heading. The loss of an unborn or newly born child is still the loss of a child; what differs is how people will react to such a death. People who would gather around and help you grieve the loss of a child may not do the same for a miscarriage or stillbirth. Society does not view a pregnancy loss in the same way it views other losses. And there is no formal venue—no wake or memorial service—in which relatives and friends can express their sorrow. The absence of public recognition can make it difficult for people to say anything at all.

Right or wrong, the reaction you receive will range from discomfort to no acknowledgment at all. Although you never had the chance to know your child, in your heart you know that he or she is a part of you nonetheless. Your grief at this death carries the same characteristics as any other grief: you may deny the loss ever happened; you may feel angry, disappointed, and sad; it may seem that every television commercial or magazine advertisement is for baby products or has a baby in it, causing you to be depressed. But you find little if any support. It will be up to you to take the initiative.

Focus on something physical.

If you are grieving a miscarriage, consider purchasing some small item, such as a statue or music box, which you can name for the child. This can serve as a symbol that a baby really did exist. This object will be the focus of your grief.

Be prepared for later grief.

The miscarriage itself will be difficult enough to process. But be aware of another date that may undo any progress you might have made in your grief journey: your baby's due date. As you approach the date on which your baby was scheduled to make his or her appearance, you will probably find that you are becoming more anxious. The whole incident will keep recurring in your mind, and you may feel that you are reliving the miscarriage. Make note of the date and prepare yourself for it. If you put the date completely out of your mind, it will sneak up on you anyway, even though you may not realize why you are feeling depressed.

Don't be afraid to create memories around your deceased child.

If your baby was stillborn or died shortly after birth, you may be comforted by rocking the baby or dressing the baby for burial. Consider asking for a handprint, footprint, or lock of hair from your child. You might even want to have a picture taken. Some people may find that distasteful, but it's better to take the picture while you can rather than not have a picture and desperately want one later.

Also make sure to invite the grandparents to hold the baby if they desire—this gesture will help them work through their grief.

Request the clothes and bedding of your newborn.

While it may not seem that this would be a necessary request, asking for the receiving blanket, clothes, warming cap, and name bracelet will help you in your grief. Each of these items will carry the scent of your newborn baby. This helps to reassure the mother that the baby actually existed.

If friends have completely ignored you, don't be afraid to phone someone and tell that person that you need to talk about your loss.

Once your friend is aware of your need to discuss your feelings, he or she may become more available to you. Most people are willing to grieve with you if they feel that it is appropriate and wanted. Much of the silence after a miscarriage or stillbirth is due to society's discomfort concerning infant loss.

Don't worry if everyday chores are not getting done.

The period that follows the loss of a child through miscarriage or premature death is probably the loneliest time you will ever have to endure. If it is within your budget, have meals delivered, employ a cleaning service, and hire a neighbor to cut the grass. Do whatever you can afford to do to make your life uncomplicated for the time being. You will return to your normal routine after you have had sufficient time to grieve your loss. But you must give yourself time to heal.

It is perfectly acceptable to permanently consider yourselves parents.

Just because your child has died does not mean that you are not a mother or a father. Whether your child was ten years old or one hour old at the time of death is irrelevant. The fact that the baby did not make it to full term is irrelevant. He or she was your child, and you are the parents.

WHEN YOU ARE DEALING WITH A LOSS THROUGH ABORTION OR ADOPTION

You may have lost a child through abortion or adoption. Regardless of your feelings, beliefs, and circumstances at the time of your decision—or even now—you will need to grieve this loss just as surely as you must grieve any other.

Many of the principles for any other grief apply as well to the loss of a child by abortion or adoption. However, both of these losses carry their own pains. Following are just a few thoughts on these sensitive matters.

You may suffer from post abortion syndrome.

You may be angry or reluctant to talk. You may be indifferent to events going on around you and you may be unable to relax. If you are married and/or mother to other children, you may find that you are unable to relate to your husband or your kids. These symptoms can last for a long time—months or even years. But if it seems that these feelings are overwhelming or you are unable to function, consider getting professional assistance from a grief counselor or other grief/medical professional.

Depending on the type of adoption you chose, the intensity and type of your grief may vary.

If you chose closed adoption, which does not allow for any further contact with your child, you will need to grieve the adoption much as you would a death. As far as you are concerned, this child is gone, although you can be comforted by knowing that he or she is being loved and cared for by others. Still, you must allow yourself the same stages and aspects of grief as you would if the child had actually died.

If you chose open adoption, which allows the birth mother contact with her child but within limits, you must still grieve your loss as a mother, because you won't be allowed that role in this child's life. However, you will have some opportunity to see this child and even have some involvement. The important thing to remember is that you will grieve, one way or another. And you have every right to grieve. In some ways, perhaps in most ways, this child is now lost to you.

You may feel that you have no right to grieve because you chose your child's outcome.

But you do. You have left behind something you had feelings (positive or negative) for. You may have made your decision out of deep love—or with little feeling at all—for your child. But you can't get him or her back. You need support. Seek it. Go to family or friends or whomever you think could help you through your grief journey. You are grieving; you deserve support.

Depending on your relationship to the child's father, you may have other issues to resolve.

Perhaps you alone made the decision to give up your child, or perhaps you and the father made it together. You may not have agreed, even if you discussed it. And you may have actually felt compelled toward your decision because of your relationship to the father. Whatever the case, chances are that this relationship is now severely strained. If the child's father is part of your family—you are married to him or are at least still on speaking terms with his family—then the tension and trouble in your relationship to him will spill into other family relationships. You may have to deal with the child's grandparents on either side of the family. These heartbreaking issues can drive a wedge into all of your relationships permanently.

It's extremely important to get professional help—for yourself, the child's father, perhaps for the entire family. No matter how good your intentions were when you made the choice to give up your child—and no matter how wise you think that decision was, your emotions are powerful and must be faced. Your grief in this situation is complex, and you need support.

WHEN YOU AND YOUR PARTNER GRIEVE IN DIFFERENT WAYS

It may seem obvious, but men and women often have different ways of grieving. For instance, some men are still not accustomed to public displays of affection or comfort, whereas some women are socialized to be more demonstrative. The differences in how husbands and wives view death and the grieving process can be substantial or subtle. It is helpful to be aware of these differences.

Men may return to their normal routines more quickly than women.

Some men may push the unpleasant experience to the back of their minds and actually believe they are over the death when, in fact, they haven't allowed themselves any time to grieve at all. Men tend to "keep busy" after the death of a loved one, particularly that of a child. Keeping a "normal" pace gives the appearance of being strong, of being able to cope. Women, on the other hand, may be forced into dealing with circumstances and loose ends resulting from the death: caring for another parent; cleaning and preparing the parents' house to be put up for sale; removing the belongings from a dead child's bedroom, and so forth. Because the wife cannot return to her normal routine, she is forced into dealing with the death and the grieving process. The husband and wife may be miles apart in their journeys through grief.

Women may be more willing than men to talk about their losses.

Because men often believe they must be self-sufficient, they may feel that they have to endure the ordeal alone, without any support group, counseling, or help from friends and relatives. Women will generally feel a need to share their experiences with someone; they are more likely than men to find someone to talk to.

Men are not expected to cry openly or lose control of the situation.

This masking of their true emotions may disrupt sleeping patterns and lead to aggressive behavior or anger later on. Men may wake suddenly in the middle of the night, talking or screaming to no one in particular. Some men may feel that they were not strong enough, smart enough, or good enough to have saved their loved one from death. To mask these feelings, husbands and fathers may ignore them and try to appear "fine." They don't want to think about the death or the grieving process. They fear that losing control in front of others may make them appear weak; they feel as if they have to tough it out and show that they can keep their emotions in check. As far as they are concerned, the weeping is for the women and children. Furthermore, men may be totally unaware of difficulties faced by other family members. It's as if, in blocking their emotions about their own pain, men block out information about pain in the lives of other family members.

Women may be perceived as incapable of handling adversity as well as men.

More women outlive their husbands than the other way around. And it is often the women who hold the family together in crisis; after all, they often manage the daily details of a household. It is still true in many households that the wife physically spends more time around the children and thus is better tuned to them emotionally. In these situations, mom is more likely than dad to deal directly with helping the children grieve. It may be the wife who holds the family together while the husband falls apart or distances himself emotionally. Because women are more likely to cry and show emotions, they are inaccurately perceived as fragile. Yet their ability to process their grief gives them an advantage over the men who may freeze emotionally during times of crisis and loss.

Because husbands are expected to be strong for their families, they are often overlooked at wakes and funerals.

Mourners who ask a man, "How is your wife holding up?" without asking him how *he* is holding up, are inadvertently telling the husband that his feelings and emotions are negligible. He may not even realize it, but feelings of anger or confusion may actually be building up within him. On the other hand, the wife may have many friends and family members outwardly showing their concerns and affection for her. This enables her to start the grieving process much earlier than her husband.

WHEN YOUR BROTHER OR SISTER HAS DIED

Whether one has lost a brother or sister, siblings grieve like no one else—including parents. Each sibling relationship is unique. One way or the other, the death of your sibling will affect you.

Mourners may ignore the grief of brothers and sisters.

Friends may think that your grief is not severe. They may decide not to attend the wake, and they may neglect to send a card or acknowledge the loss in any way. Those people who do come to pay their respects may actually fail to offer condolences to you and your other brothers or sisters, mistakenly believing that your grief is not as intense as that of your parents (or, if the sibling was married, his or her spouse and children). They will comment about how worried they are about your parents and how much your parents have had to endure. If this happens, you are bound to feel slighted. You and your remaining brothers and sisters may be trying to shield your parents from the pain of grief. But that doesn't negate your own pain. Just try to remember that the people who forgot about you had good intentions but not good information or understanding.

Grief for a brother or sister may be more intense than anyone can imagine.

If you really admired your brother or sister, you may feel totally abandoned now that he or she is gone. Even adults often feel lost after the death of a sibling. Brothers and sisters know each other like no one else. You may have shared remembrances of days gone by or little secrets that were known by only the two of you. You, in particular, may have been closest to the deceased because the two of you were closer in age or spent more time together than with other family members. The closeness of this relationship will both comfort you and cause you pain when that sibling dies. Your grief will be very strong indeed. You may be losing not only a brother or sister but also a close friend. Allow yourself to experience this sadness.

And even if others think you shouldn't be so deeply affected, don't allow their attitudes to cause you guilt for your own pain.

Surviving siblings, especially teenagers, may try to emulate their deceased brother or sister.

It is not uncommon for a teenager to try to copy aspects of a deceased sibling's life. Being with his or her friends or doing things that the brother or sister did can help a surviving sibling feel closer to the person who is now gone. If this is the case for you, be careful of extremes. If, for instance, your brother excelled in high-school football but soccer is more your sport, don't give up playing soccer to pursue football. Most likely you will not have the same measure of success as did your brother. Rather, try to imitate his dedication to the sport. Use his routine for practicing or the way he approached each game. That way you will be honoring your brother but still pursuing your own sport.

Watch for signs that remaining siblings are acting differently.

In order to escape the reality and pain of losing their brother or sister, teenagers may become reckless. They may start taking drugs, driving carelessly, or hanging around a rougher crowd. If you find yourself doing any of these things, try talking with a friend or counselor.

Parents take note: If your children are displaying any of these behaviors, seek professional counseling.

Adolescents often feel that they have to compensate for the loss of their sibling.

You may find yourself trying to fill the gaps left by your deceased brother or sister. You may also feel that you must take care of your parents, sparing them any more pain. A teenager may actually try to be the parent to the parents. Remember that it is not your job to be grief manager for your parents or to become their caretakers.

Parents take note: While it may be of some relief to have your children take care of you during this time of loss, beware of the emotional risk. If you lean too heavily on your remaining children, they will be unable to do their own grieving. Seek balance as you support your children and as they support you.

Teens may want to talk to people other than their parents about their grief.

This can be a healthy strategy because your parents, too, are grieving. Don't hesitate to approach pastors, counselors, neighbors, aunts and uncles, or your peers for the support you need.

Parents take note: Don't take it personally if your children do not confide in you during this time of loss. Your young adults may want to spare you any further pain or burden. In addition, they are at an age where confiding in a parent is just not cool, even about something as close as the death of a sibling. Respect their decision and be glad that they are talking about their pain with someone else rather than keeping it inside.

The dynamics of the family may change as a result of the death.

Each member of a household has a particular role in the hierarchy of the nuclear family. If the deceased sibling was the member who kept the family together or who always had the holiday gatherings or who always planned the family vacations, the duties of each survivor will now be altered. For instance, it might now fall upon you to uphold family tradition by having the Thanksgiving dinner at your house. While it is perfectly acceptable for you to take on a responsibility that once belonged to your deceased brother or sister, you need to do so for the right reasons. It is in his or her memory that you are carrying on the torch. But make the celebration on your own terms. It's a mistake to try to replicate exactly the manner in which your sibling performed the function; attempting to do so may actually make everyone more uncomfortable.

WHEN YOUR CLOSE FRIEND HAS DIED

Friends are unique individuals. They don't come with our families but are chosen by us to be a part of our lives. Friends can be closer than brothers and sisters and even parents and children. We love them voluntarily, not because we are supposed to. They can be our confidantes and our support systems. To further complicate the issue, just when we need our friend the most for support, he or she is not there. There may be no one to turn to for emotional encouragement. And to make matters worse, many

people will wonder exactly why you are grieving at all—
after all, you're not a family member!

If you are mourning the loss of a close friend, don't feel you need to explain your loss to anyone.

No one will understand the relationship between you and your friend. The bond between the two of you may have been unspoken but strong nonetheless. You will need to realize that the emotional support is not there for you. It will be up to you to gather that reinforcement from new and untried sources. Spouses, parents, children—all of whom you may never have confided in regarding certain matters—may now need to be called upon for assistance. Grief support groups may be a viable—and valuable—alternative for filling the void created by the death of your friend. Other options include individual counseling, local clergy, and medical professionals. While your friend cannot be replaced, it is important to find someone to help you through your healing process.

Although you are hurting deeply, do remember to consider your friend's family at this sad time.

This may be a form of grief management: your grief taking a back seat to theirs. Give any assistance you think appropriate to the surviving spouse; offer emotional support to any children. Remember to console any surviving parents—whom you may have known for many years—and stay with them if they are sitting alone at the wake or service. They will appreciate your kindness.

Remember that most companies do not allow paid days off for the death of a person who is not a member of your family.

You may have to take a vacation day or a day with no pay in order to attend the funeral of your friend. But take it; don't consider not attending. Being there will help you through your loss, and your friend's family will appreciate it.

After the funeral, offer to help the surviving family members complete any task you knew your friend had in progress.

Or, you may offer to perform temporarily any chore that you knew was your friend's responsibility. Gradually, you will be able to turn over this duty to a family member.

WHEN YOUR PET HAS DIED

Your pet may be as close—or even closer—to you as a friend or family member. For those couples who are without kids, pets may be a substitute for children. Pets—whether dogs or cats, birds or fish—fulfill a special role in the home. They offer unconditional love. The death of a pet is a loss that brings sadness to all who loved the pet. There will be a grieving process, although it usually does not last as long as that following the death of a human. If it is your desire to do so, it's OK to have a funeral. A funeral will bring closure to the death.

If you have children, be sure to use this experience for teaching them about death. (See chapter 4, "Children and

Grief," for more suggestions on helping children deal with the death of a pet.)

You may need to have your pet put to sleep.

There are numerous reasons that you may need to consider having a pet put to sleep. Sometimes old age or chronic illness is the issue. Sometimes a pet becomes dangerous to family members, visitors, and neighbors.

The entire family should participate in this decision. Every member of the family must be allowed to express his or her opinion. Consideration must be made for the pet's condition (is the pet in pain? is the pet losing control of bodily functions? is the pet starting to snap at you?) as well as the feelings of the children. In all likelihood your children will express their love for the pet and their unwillingness to part with it. If a consensus cannot be reached, make an appointment with your veterinarian. Discuss the pros and cons of keeping the pet alive and of putting the pet to sleep. Children may better understand the gravity of the situation if explained to them by a "professional" rather than by a parent.

If your pet dies from natural causes or as the result of an accident, watch for signs of guilt in your children.

They may feel that they neglected the pet, thus causing its death. Take time to explain to them that they are not responsible and reassure them again and again. If your explanations do not seem to help, then consider a session with a member of the clergy or a grief counselor.

Planning the funeral for your pet can be as simple as a shoebox burial in the backyard or as intricate as a formal funeral service at a pet cemetery.

The most important aspect of this ceremony is to make sure that your children participate. Have the children choose the burial box, something soft for the inside of the box, and a cover to protect the box. During the service, each child can say something they liked about the pet, sing a song together, and say goodbye. Or you may consider having the child write a farewell letter to the pet, which can then be buried with the pet.

Do not think that you are going overboard with your pet funeral.

You will be demonstrating the respect that any death of a living creature deserves and demands. You will also be preparing your children to deal with the death of a loved one, and you will be helping them through their grief. But you must stay within your means. Don't go over your budget to have a funeral at a pet cemetery.

WHEN YOU ARE GRIEVING BUT HAVE GONE BACK TO WORK

A good number of companies today are living at least fifty years in the past regarding grief policies. It is assumed that because wakes, which used to last three days, now last only a day, fewer days are necessary for funeral leave. Companies fail to take into account that some people have to travel maybe thousands of miles for a wake and funeral.

And the notion that employees may actually need time to adjust to their loss and begin a journey through grief is only now beginning to establish itself. Know any bereavement policy your company may have in place.

Beware that most places of business provide employees with only three paid days of leave for the death of a family member, regardless of the relationship.

Consider taking additional time off as necessary beyond the allotted three days. If you have used all your vacation time for the year, consider talking to your supervisor about taking a short, unpaid leave. This time off may be even more important to your well-being, especially if you have used up vacation time caring for, or being with, your loved one during a prolonged illness or in the final days.

Talk to your supervisor about any difficulties you may be experiencing in performing your job responsibilities.

Discuss the possibility of reducing your hours of work for a few days; see if there is a way to lessen your workload. Ask if there is a private place you might use if you need to be alone for a few minutes during the workday. Make your boss aware that focus, memory, sleep patterns, and concentration may be affected by your loss. You may even lose the ability to make decisions or be unable to understand everyday details of your regular job.

If coworkers shared your workload in your absence, remember to thank them.

Be sure to make them aware of any problems you are experiencing that may affect their duties. Have lunch with them and discuss any issue you might have regarding your grief. If possible or desirable, find one good listener who can help support you during the workday.

Take advantage of any support groups, counselors, or therapists provided by your company.

The medical benefits programs at some companies are now allowing for group family counseling; help in dealing with grief and for sorting out your feelings may be a mere phone call away. Make use of the programs. And don't let work overwhelm you.

Arrange a meeting with the appropriate people to discuss any changes in insurance coverage, health insurance, pension plans, and so forth.

It is important to have the correct coverage. You may find that the differences in cost will affect your monthly income.

WHEN YOUR COWORKER OR EMPLOYEE IS GRIEVING

If you are the boss or supervisor, do not put undue pressure on the bereaved.

Do not bring up work issues at the wake or funeral, although you may be tempted to ask, "When are you coming back to work?" or "Where is the Jones report you were working on?" If you need information, get it at another time. Be supportive. If it's within your authority to do so, give grieving employees the time they need. Understand that, upon their return to work, the quality and/or quantity of work may be temporarily diminished. Do not assign new duties. Work with them on keeping things as simple as possible for a little while until they are up to maintaining a full workload. Consider the possibility of offering employees the option to work at home until they have organized a new home schedule to conform to any new situations arising from the death. A caring and understanding boss will be appreciated and go a long way in cementing employee/boss relations.

If you are a coworker, be understanding and offer to help however you can.

Consider taking on a little of your coworker's workload, if permissible. Acknowledge the loss by attending the wake and/or funeral. Tell other coworkers about the death. When your coworker returns to work, recognize that he or she is grieving. Be a good listener and understand that the bereaved may talk and/or act differently. His or her demeanor may be moody or extremely negative. This is not a reflection of how he or she feels about you. It is merely the grieving process at work. It may take weeks or even months before your fellow worker returns to normal. Do not give up on your colleague or abandon him or her when that person is most in need of friendship and understanding.

WHEN YOU HAVE NO LOVE FOR THE DECEASED

Situations do occur when someone closely related to you dies, but there is no love between the two of you. The only emotional tie you might have had with that person was strictly that of kinship. Whether due to years of childhood abuse—emotional, sexual, or physical— or to years of marital infidelity, your love for that person has long since disappeared.

You may actually be glad that the person is no longer in your life.

The only feelings you have regarding this person's death may be relief. You may be saying to yourself, *Good riddance!* You may even be glad this person is finally out of your life. Yet society says that you must be sad and grieve. Because of this, you may start to feel guilty for not having the proper feelings at this time of loss. Of course it is best to show respect to the deceased in public situations—for the sake of others who cared for that person and for the sake of children or siblings. But do not feel guilty for your lack of grief. Whatever the reason for your mind-set, you do not have to justify your feelings to anybody. Only you know all about the events that transpired between you and the deceased and how that relationship has affected your life.

Your time at the wake and funeral may be awkward.

Since a substantial number of people may be unaware of your true feelings, they will be extending their heartfelt condolences to you. Accept them graciously. A simple

"Thank you" will suffice. There is no need to tell everyone at this time the truth about the deceased. If you feel compelled to tell someone, wait until after the burial for the proper setting and the proper time.

You will need to bring your relationship to closure.

Even though there was no love lost, you will still need to grieve the death. You need to verbalize all of your negative feelings. Whether before the wake or after, single out another family member or friend in which to confide. Choose someone who, if he or she doesn't feel the same way toward the deceased as you do, at least understands why you feel as you do. Talk about the events that influenced your life. Express your anger, your hate, your rage; shout, yell, or scream, if you need to. Take as much time as necessary to complete this undertaking. And when choosing a spot in which to do this, make sure you are in a safe place for the task—somewhere isolated where no one else will hear your words. People are uncomfortable talking "ill of the dead," and if they hear you speaking in a negative way, they will probably judge you rather than sympathize.

4 | Children and Grief

I shall not forget you.
Look, I have engraved you
   on the palms of my hands.

Isaiah 49:15–16

HOW SAD it is when children must learn about death for the very first time. All at once they are confronted with the loss of someone dear, forced to face sadness and crying all around, and compelled to deal with strangers and people who are only vaguely familiar to them. Their routines are disrupted, and they wonder why they are feeling so unhappy. They may have taken a first step toward adulthood, but what a price they have paid.

HOW TO TALK TO CHILDREN ABOUT DEATH

Any child, of any age, at any time can suddenly be thrust into the grieving process by the death of a parent. When you consider the number of children who will suffer through the divorce of their parents, you can begin to see just how many children are journeying through grief before they reach the age of eighteen. Helping a child through his or her journey through grief is an undertaking of utmost importance with significant ramifications and tremendous rewards.

When death does enter the lives of your children, don't keep the truth from them.

Children need to know the circumstances surrounding the loss of a loved one and the reason for any change in routine. Knowledge concerning the death makes it less scary to children. Being kept in the dark causes their imagination to run wild. What they are fantasizing about could actually be worse than the truth. Be specific about what will happen to the deceased's body. Tell those who will be taking care of your children in the immediate future (if they are not going to attend the wake) to answer questions truthfully and completely. If your children will be attending the service, tell them about the room where they will be, what they will be expected to do, what they should expect to see and hear, who will be sitting with them, and what other people may do (cry, pray, reminisce).

Define terms.

Remember that children may be confused by euphemisms such as "going away" or "passed on." Don't be afraid to use the word "dead." Make time to explain funeral terms. Explain that "the body" refers to the deceased's entire head and body (not just a torso); that "looks like they are sleeping" (or putting a pet "to sleep") is not the same as the sleep they have at night or during naps; and that "a wake" is just a term for visiting the deceased at the funeral home and that the deceased won't actually be "awake." Also, explain that although the bottom half of the deceased's body may not be seen, it is there and has not been removed. Prepare them for the fact that the body will be cold and firm to the touch, the eyes will be closed, and there will be no movement. Listen for other unfamiliar words and phrases so that you may explain. If you need assistance, the social services department of your local hospital has considerable resources available for dealing with death and children. Clergy from your church can also be called upon to help you explain death to a child.

Be open, available, and truthful in discussions about death.

Don't be afraid to show your own feelings of grief in front of the children. Your emotions of sadness and anger will reassure children that it is permissible to have these feelings. Answer only the questions that are posed to you, so as not to overwhelm children with too much information. Understand that young children (under age six) may not accept that death is final. Encourage kids to talk, write, or draw about their feelings and their fears.

In trying to educate children about death, try to remember your own earliest memories about death.

Remember your own questions, fears, and impressions as a child. Try to recall the first wake or funeral you attended, what you learned from this experience, and what impact seeing a dead person had upon you. Share these memories with your child.

Don't be surprised that children may be better able to talk about death than you are.

Be prepared to answer such questions as

- "Why?"
- "What's going to happen to me?"
- "Did I do something wrong?"
- "Does it hurt to die?"
- "Can a person be replaced?"
- "What happens to the dead person's body after it's buried?"
- "What happens if I cry?"
- "Do I have to cry?"
- "Why did God make my daddy die?"
- "When is mommy coming back?"
- "How long will grandma be away?"
- "Do I have to look at grandpa?"
- "Can I touch the dead person?"

HOW TO HELP CHILDREN DEAL WITH DEATH

Teaching a child about dying, death, and grief is certainly not an easy task. You must first explore your own feelings about death. It will be all the more difficult to explain these complicated issues to children if you have not come to grips with the issues yourself.

Take advantage of common events to prepare children for their first encounter with death in the family.

Talk freely about life cycles in plants and animals. Whenever an arrangement of flowers is no longer alive, take the opportunity to talk about the flowers, how they were once alive and are now dead. If you plant a garden, discuss the seasons of planting, growing, and harvesting of crops and plants. If you purchase a new pet or have to put a pet to sleep, discuss the birth, life, and death cycles of pets—and humans.

Approach each child as an individual when it comes to facing wakes and funerals.

There is no specific age at which children should be considered old enough to attend a wake and/or funeral. A four year old who was extremely close to the deceased or who is extremely sensitive and responsive to the moods of others may actually be more ready to attend than a nine year old who is a little immature or who really doesn't care. Consider the emotional stability and maturity of the child and the impact it may have on him or her before making your decision. Make sure you have spent adequate time explaining death and the surrounding circumstances of a wake and funeral. But do not worry that having a child attend the wake will have negative effects later in his or her life. There are far more adults who have psychological problems because they were *prevented* from attending a wake and saying goodbye than there are adults who were damaged because they attended the wake or funeral.

Don't force children to attend wakes or funerals, but don't keep them from attending if they wish.

If they are adamantly opposed to going, imediately take the time to discuss it with them. This will allow the children to express their fears and emotions. It is also an opportunity to lessen any possible misconceptions they have about death. And such a discussion can ward off possible future grief and guilt due to a child's decision to be absent at the funeral. Children's attendance will often strengthen their impressions that family and life go on, even after a death. Their attendance can also help them face the reality of death and adjust to the future.

Don't be surprised if children have nightmares or bed-wetting problems in the days and months following the death of a loved one.

There may be bouts of depression, denial, anger, withdrawal, obnoxious behavior, stomachaches, or silliness. These symptoms occur when children do not yet have the skills to express their feelings adequately. Also, they may not want to upset you anymore or cause you additional pain. They may become clingy, always wanting to be near you. This may stem from their fear that you will die and leave them alone. In particular, don't downplay any feelings of guilt that children may express, thus preventing them from sharing those feelings. Rather, keep stressing that the death was in no way their fault. If they are having difficulty sleeping, keep a night-light on. Sometimes it's best to allow a distressed child to sleep in the same room or bed as you. If, after a reasonable time has passed, the child has not been able to deal with these nighttime struggles, counseling should be sought.

One word of caution: Remember that children may overhear your telephone conversations with friends, family, or coworkers. While you may need an outlet to express your feelings, frustrations, and anger, what your children hear you say over the telephone may be confusing or upsetting to them.

Be sure to give quality time to your children as they work through their grief.

Reassure them, hug them, and tell them that you love them. Be sensitive to their feelings and try to analyze the meaning of any peculiar statements they might make. What are they really trying to say—or not say? You must accept the fact that individual children will probably grieve differently, and all of them will grieve differently from you.

As important as quality time is, children won't grieve on a schedule. It's best to actually spend more time with your children during periods of loss. If you are close by much of the time, you will be there when the waves of fear, sadness, and anger crash unexpectedly.

HOW TO HELP CHILDREN GRIEVE THE DEATH OF A PARENT

Discuss your spouse's role in the family and how that void will be filled.

Explain that the deceased parent will be missed and cannot be replaced but explain further that certain household chores may now be reassigned. Be sure to avoid the appearance that a child will be replacing the deceased parent.

Watch for signs that your child is being taunted.

Often, children can be extremely cruel. They will look at the surviving child, feel that a child without a parent makes that child unusual, and begin to taunt him or her. Be aware of any change in your child's behavior that may have been precipitated by such an incident.

Plan family time together.

A trip, movie, or outing may be in order. Or you could spend time together remembering the deceased. Activities could include writing letters to the deceased, drawing pictures of the deceased or pictures that the deceased would liked to have seen. Record on audio- or videotape your thoughts about the life—and death—of the deceased. These steps are creative as well as therapeutic.

Plan ahead for holidays and anniversaries.

Discuss together how each person would like to observe the event at hand. Use this time to see if your children have any particular fears or concerns in dealing with their emotions and the upcoming event.

Reassure your children that they will not be left alone.

Use this occasion to update your will to reflect the loss of your spouse. Draw up a new one if necessary, but be sure to name someone who will take care of your children in the event that something happens to you.

HOW TO HELP CHILDREN GRIEVE THE DEATH OF A SIBLING

Children and older adolescents may actually feel responsible for their sibling's death.

They may have been angry at their brother or sister at the time of death and therefore feel that they are to blame. While they should be reassured that any emotion— including guilt—is permissible, your children must also be told that being mad at someone cannot cause that person to die. Parents should try to help their surviving children resolve any feelings of guilt by encouraging them to talk about their dead brother or sister.

Children must know that it is OK to have fun again.

They can go out with friends again and even laugh again. They can participate in sports or other activities without feeling guilty. It is also acceptable to take up a hobby, craft, or sport that was previously associated with the deceased sibling. This can be a great way to honor his or her memory and may actually make the surviving child feel closer to the deceased. But care must be taken to make the hobby or craft or sport their own and not a mere imitation of what their brother or sister did.

Children may feel lost without their brother or sister.

Perhaps the deceased child was the hero of the family or the one looked up to by the other children. Or perhaps it was the deceased child who played with or was confided in by a particular brother or sister. That surviving child is now alone. Even with twelve other siblings, it may be the relationship between the child in question and the deceased that was the strongest and that may have been held in the highest regard by the surviving sibling. For two siblings who were particularly close, care must be taken that the remaining child not stay in a shell for any length of time, not fall in with the wrong type of friends, or not start taking drugs or alcohol. All are real possibilities. If depression continues, a doctor should be consulted, and a grief counselor or group should be considered.

HOW TO HELP CHILDREN GRIEVE THE DEATH OF A PET

Do not minimize the impact that the death of a pet can have on a child. It can be devastating. For a child, that pet may have been a friend or, at the very least, a source of security.

Planning a funeral for your pet can be the first step in helping your child start the grieving process.

This gives the child the opportunity to say goodbye to someone who has been an important part of his or her life. A pet funeral gives closure to the child's loss, gives the child some sense of control of the situation, and most important, allows the child to begin grieving. Choosing a box in which to bury the pet is a good first step to getting the child involved. Having the child decorate the box with pictures that have a special meaning compels the child to think more about the loss. It also helps to have the child verbalize at the funeral service what he or she liked about the pet. Naming special qualities about the pet forces the child to think about the pet and focus on the loss. Even toddlers can start the grieving process by coloring a picture. It doesn't have to be a picture of the pet but some picture the pet would like; this can be folded up and put in the box with the pet. Dealing with the death of the pet helps a child start the healing process.

Some children may want a picture of the pet.

Do not discourage this. You can snap a picture and then hold onto it after the pet's burial. Chances are the child may never ask to see it again. But if your child does want to see it, it will be there. This is not really a morbid request. It is a request by a young person to have a special memory of his or her pet to treasure.

Consider removing articles that were associated with the pet.

Dog chains, water bowls, and cages should be removed and stored. Include toys, balls, and anything that might serve as a sad reminder of the pet. Decide together where the articles should be kept, but make sure they are not in sight. For the first few weeks, seeing these reminders might make some children extremely sad.

Replace rituals.

Changing the routine of your children may be an important step in their healing process. If, for instance, your children always took the dog for a walk after dinner, help fill the void with some other activity: play a game, go for a bicycle ride, or read a book together. Having some activity in the time frame that was usually reserved for the pet will help children move forward and achieve closure.

Watch for sudden signs of crying in your child.

Be aware that your children might be watching programs on television or coming upon pictures in their magazines and books that remind them of their beloved pet. It is impossible to know when a commercial or advertisement will suddenly trigger sadness and crying in your child. If you are not aware, you might see them with tears in their eyes and not know why. But if you know that an ad or a commercial may have precipitated the event, you can use the circumstances to draw out the emotions being felt by the child.

Help your children grasp that death is final.

Your child may believe that if he or she prays hard enough to God the pet may come back to life. Explain as often as necessary that death is final and that pets—as well as humans—do not come back from the dead.

Do not immediately replace your child's dead pet with a new animal.

To do so sends a message that it is all right to forget about your loss and the sadness associated with it. Your child should be allowed to miss the pet and to mourn its loss.

Watch for signs of lasting depression in your child.

While it is perfectly all right for children to be sad for a short while after the death of a pet, they must not remain downcast for more than a couple of weeks. Explain that the pet would not have wanted them to mope around and do nothing; that it is OK to go out with friends again, and it's all right to have fun. If the depression continues, consider going to a grief counselor or support group for children.

5 | Violent and Unexpected Deaths

'I am sending an angel to precede you, to guard you as you go and bring you to the place that I have prepared.'

Exodus 23:20

WHEN A LOVED ONE dies unexpectedly from natural causes, there is shock as well as disbelief. But if that same loved one is killed in an accident, has been the victim of a murder or a nationwide crisis, or has committed suicide, the trauma is even more troubling to the family. The whole set of circumstances surrounding the death compounds the loss.

WHEN YOUR LOVED ONE HAS COMMITTED SUICIDE

Suicide crosses all boundaries of age, race, religion, and socioeconomic status. For children as young as five and into the early teens, suicide is the sixth leading cause of death. For older teenagers and young adults up to the age of twenty-four, suicide ranks number three. For the survivors of suicide victims, the death itself is devastating enough. But that devastation is often compounded by the survivors' belief that the death was preventable.

You will probably feel that you could have prevented this death.

"If only I had been there." This is a frequent lament of the survivors of a suicide. Family and friends are flooded with feelings that they somehow failed the person who has taken his or her own life. They inaccurately believe that being with the loved one somehow would have prevented the suicide. What most survivors fail to realize—but must come to terms with—is the fact that their loved one had his or her own agenda. It is impossible to be with your loved one every minute of every day. If someone intends to end his or her life, it will happen. The day and time may change because you or someone else was present at a particular time. But it will occur, sooner or later, if that is the choice. You could not have prevented it.

You will probably suffer from survivor's guilt.

When people live through natural disasters such as floods and fires, or through mass tragedies such as plane crashes, they often wonder why they lived while others perished. This sort of guilt accompanies survivors of a suicide as well. You will wonder why you were able to deal with life and manage to keep living while your loved one could not. Perhaps you and the loved one suffered some of the same struggles. Why is he dead but you're not?

Be aware that these feelings are normal in this situation. It will not help to replay and second-guess. You will never understand fully why this happened. If your guilt feelings persist, seek help from a counselor or support group.

It is common to feel hurt, anger, resentment, and rejection.

When a loved one chooses to remove himself from your life, you can't help but feel angry and rejected to some degree. It can help to remind yourself that most people who take their own lives are not well at the time. They are often emotionally overwhelmed, if not mentally ill or physically debilitated. All of us are less wise when we make choices under such circumstances. So, while your loved one chose to end his life, he was not at his best when he made the choice. It is likely that he was unable to be rational at all.

Nevertheless, you will resent what this person's choice has done to your life. Accept your anger, resentment, and feelings of rejection as valid responses to the situation. You may need a counselor's help in working through these feelings. You may need a suicide survivor support group.

It is common for family members to feel shame.

Society has attached a certain stigma to suicide. This can make it difficult to tell others the truth about what has happened to your loved one. It can be tempting to deny the truth altogether. You and other family members may try to conceal the actual cause of death.

In keeping the matter a secret, you can delay or prolong the grieving process. It takes a lot of energy to keep details from slipping out. This is not healthy nor is it necessary. In general, people are far more understanding about this matter than in earlier decades. The causes of depression and suicide are well published in books and magazines and often the subject of television and radio programs.

To those people who are not understanding, don't bother to offer an explanation. A person's life has ended; there is no need to dwell on the why or how. Tell people what you feel they need to know and what you feel comfortable having made known. Then move on to begin your recovery.

Family and friends will regret missing the signals that a loved one was contemplating suicide.

Again, we must stress that when a person is intent on ending his or her life, there's not much anyone can do. Sometimes there are signals, but sometimes there aren't. And all signals are easier to see in hindsight. At the time it can be very difficult to see that someone is trying to say good-bye. You may fail to notice certain signs, such as your loved one giving things away or uncharacteristically hugging you good-bye after a friendly get-together. What you may consider to be a normal comment in conversation may actually have meant much more. But you cannot read another person's mind.

You still have to say good-bye.

Because suicides are sudden, there is usually no time to say goodbye. You need to find a way to bring this matter to closure. Write a letter, stating how you feel: betrayed, angry, bewildered, frustrated, shocked. Say whatever you need to get off your chest. Spend time talking to other family members about all the good times you spent together—and, yes, even the bad times. Commiserating together can be comforting.

WHEN YOUR LOVED ONE HAS BEEN MURDERED

During the final two decades of the last century, nearly a half million people were murdered in the United States. These deaths have touched millions of people across the country, either directly or indirectly.

It's important to grasp the situation as soon as possible.

Hearing the news of a loved one's murder is devastating and disorienting. You may refuse to believe what you're being told by police or others. You will say that it just cannot be possible. The sheer horror of the death is incomprehensible. But it is important to grasp (and help others grasp) the situation as quickly as possible. Not only will you have to deal with the usual matters surrounding any death, but you may have to talk with police and answer questions—many times. It is imperative to give the authorities as much information as promptly as you can; this will increase their odds of catching the murderer.

Understand that a murder creates an unreal atmosphere and that people will act strangely.

Family and friends may immediately stop verbalizing your loved one's name. You may have to deal with the media, who will be pressuring you for comment or asking you painful and thoughtless questions. You will have to cope with curiosity seekers who want to see the family or the scene of the crime. There could be numerous spectators standing or sitting around, damaging your private property. And, because of all the disrespect around you, you may feel mistreated and ignored by the "system," whether the case goes forward or not. To help you deal with all these elements, it may be wise to enlist a friend or family member to serve as a grief manager.

Don't be surprised when your own reactions are extreme.

As a member of the victim's family, you will be looking for the truth about what happened to your loved one. Sooner or later, you will want to know if and how he or she suffered. You will want to know exactly what happened and why the murderer chose your loved one as his or her victim. Don't be surprised if you or other family members become obsessed with the details of the crime and with finding the killer.

You will also be dealing with rage on many levels. You may want to personally search for the murderer or even start thinking of ways to actually kill the murderer if you have the opportunity. You will feel oppressed and abused by the crime-solving process itself. You'll tire of answering the same questions again and again, and you'll be angry when investigators are not entirely forthcoming with information. You will be angry about how confusing the situation is and how impossible it is for you and your family to grasp it.

During all of this emotional turmoil, keep people around you who will help maintain balance. Don't rely on police or other authorities to give you support—their primary concern is to solve the crime, and they will be unable to help you in other ways. Go to clergy, close friends, and counselors for your equilibrium.

In time, you will want to find some way to extinguish the fire in your soul. Whether or not the crime is solved, you will need to get past your rage. And the best way to do that is to join a support group. No one can better understand your feelings than someone who has had a similar experience. If there are no support groups in your area, start one (see chapter 7). If you live in a small town and there are no other people in your area who have similar experiences, contact other victims' families in your general area. Writing them or calling them can offer comfort to you.

Be sure to say good-bye.

Because the murder of your loved one happened without any warning, you were not given the chance to say good-bye. To bring some measure of comfort to you and your family, find a way to do this. All of you need closure, whether or not the crime is solved and regardless of how long it takes.

Write a letter to your loved one. Express not only your love and how you treasured your life together but also your anger, hate, bewilderment, and shock. Spend time talking to other family members, hugging one another and crying together. Having others to share your sorrow will be of some comfort.

If you are a relative of a murder victim, your grief can last for years.

Closure may take a long while to achieve. The murderer must be apprehended, he or she must be indicted, a trial may be moved further and further back before convening, appeals will keep the matter going for years. As with the Oklahoma City bombing, it was more than six years before justice (in the eyes of many of the victims' families) was served. And even that was much speedier than others due to the bomber's decision to waive appeals. For those perpetrators sentenced to long terms in prison, parole hearings may be held periodically, forcing you to attend and testify. Justice moves slowly; your journey through grief will move just as slowly.

WHEN YOUR LOVED ONE HAS DIED IN AN ACCIDENT

In 1999, there were 41,611 fatalities as the result of automobile accidents. For people aged six through twenty-seven, car accidents are the leading cause of death; for teenagers ages fifteen through nineteen, 36 percent of all deaths are due to automobile accidents. Approximately 2,400 people in thirty-nine separate airline crashes involving American carriers were killed between January 1982 and January 2000. Add to that number the people who were killed in other types of accidents—trains, boats, construction—and firefighters and police killed in the line of duty, and you have a substantial number of grieving families trying to cope with sudden and violent loss.

You will probably experience various symptoms of shock when you learn that a loved one has died in an accident.

Your emotions may freeze up. You will deny that the accident ever happened. You will appear normal, but you will not be remembering or comprehending anything going on around you. You will appear to be listening, but in actuality you will be hearing little or none of what people are saying to you. Your mind will be reacting to the horror of all the details of the accident. You will be struggling to comprehend the physical and emotional pain suffered by your loved one during the last moments of his or her life. You may startle easily.

As best you can, communicate with other people. You need to talk, scream, cry, curse—anything to help process your shock. Other family members and friends need to do this as well. Try to be aware of more fragile family members—such as grandparents with heart or blood pressure problems—and gather people to sit and talk with them.

In some cases, help will be provided to you during this crisis time. For instance, immediately after a plane crash, most airlines assign staff members to be with victims' families to assist them in numerous ways. Clergy are on hand immediately. And, in situations where groups of people have died, there is often the added support that victims' families find in one another. As awful as it is for many people to die at once, a natural bonding occurs in these situations because so many people are suffering the same grief at the same time. Immediately, there is a support group on hand. Victims' families can ask one another questions they could not ask otherwise: Where were you when you heard about it? Why was your loved one on the plane?

Because deaths by accident occur so suddenly, there is usually no chance for good-bye.

The trauma surrounding the accident makes closure extremely difficult, especially if the body is not recoverable or if it is so severely mutilated that it cannot be viewed. Surviving relatives of those who have died in crashes have found it comforting to leave flowers at the site as a symbolic gesture. Families are often drawn to the place where their loved one was last alive. They will keep going back to try and reason why their loved one was taken so horribly and suddenly. The families of the victims of the Oklahoma City bombing keep returning to the memorial that now stands on the site of the bombing. They find the name of their loved one on one of the memorial chairs (one for each victim), and use it as a focus for their grief.

Feelings of "survivor's guilt" can be strong.

This is especially true if a last-minute change in plans caused you or another family member to be absent when the accident occurred. You wonder how it is that you're still living; you should have been there and perished with your loved one. You're alive and your loved one is dead; it isn't fair. Do your best to reject feelings of guilt. You didn't cause the accident, and you didn't decide that your loved one should die and that you should live. Survivor's guilt is very difficult to deal with, and it will take time for you to work through it. Be gentle on yourself. These feelings are normal but you will work through them and begin to heal.

WHEN A LOVED ONE HAS DIED AS THE RESULT OF A NATIONAL DISASTER

December 7, 1941: Japanese Bomb Pearl Harbor. October 17, 1989: San Francisco Suffers Major Earthquake. August 24, 1992: Hurricane Andrew Ravages Florida. April 19, 1995: Oklahoma City Bombing. September 11, 2001: World Trade Center and Pentagon Attacked by Terrorists.

Devastating headlines. So many lives lost. So much property destroyed. When a nationwide emergency strikes, the immensity of the event magnifies the individual pain associated with each calamity. A nation stands stunned, but in the midst of the chaos and confusion families must deal with their deeply personal pain. Families know that these victims are not merely faceless fatalities; they are fathers and mothers, husbands and wives, sons and daughters. Each family must cope not only with the death of a loved one, but also with the watchful eyes of the media and the whole country.

Waiting for news about your loved one will seem like an eternity.

When news of the event first breaks, you will immediately start a mental count of your family's whereabouts. Could they have been traveling on the collapsed freeway? Was their house destroyed? Where was their meeting supposed to be held? Once you have realized that your loved one could be a victim, panic or shock may set in. Emotions may range from numbness and sadness to fear and anxiety. You may experience extreme loss of concentration or find it difficult to focus on anything else but the tragedy. You may even become fixated with the constant replaying on television of the incident itself or on the devastation and disorder it caused. And all the while you will be listening and watching for any news about your loved one, hoping and praying for his or her safety.

You will need to comfort your children in the midst of your own sorrow.

When you talk about the event to your children, be as straightforward with them as possible. Be honest and use terms that are clear, concise, and accurate. Watch the television coverage with them—hugging them while reassuring them they are safe—but limit the time you watch the news together. Understand that they may need to ask the same questions over and over. Console and assure in the best way that you are able.

The urge to race to the scene may be overwhelming.

Before you arrange to go to the site of the crisis, be sure to give yourself a little time to react. Seek support from someone who will be able to help you through this terrible time and assist you with whatever immediate details need to be made. Maybe a neighbor or friend can act as a grief manager, answering the questions from media, which will most likely come.

You will need to be with others.

This compulsion to be with others suffering from the same tragedy was vividly demonstrated during the terrorist assaults of September 11, 2001. Within thirty-six hours of the attack, New York City and the State of New York had set up a nearby armory for families of possible victims. This gave the families—many of whom were clamoring for more information—a place to go where they could get updated information, share emotions, and receive grief counseling.

Expect to be overwhelmed at the site of the disaster.

Once you are there in person to witness for yourself the destruction and disarray, the pain will now increase substantially. You will try to imagine the pain your loved one has endured. You will bristle at the questions you will need to answer about your loved one: What was his height and weight? What color were her eyes? What was he wearing? Did she have any distinctive jewelry? What was her shoe size? Did he have any tattoos? You may need to provide a picture of your loved one. And, if the bodies of the victims are not immediately identifiable, you may have to secure dental records or provide a toothbrush or hair brush for DNA sampling. All these requests may be devastating to you, but they are necessary and you must assist with the requests if at all possible.

If you are supporting someone touched by a national tragedy, there are things you can do to help.

First and foremost, listen. Be there for the person in need. Assist however you can. Offer to be a grief manager or to help with any travel arrangements. If you live close enough, help with rescue efforts. Donate blood. Help coordinate any such relief efforts. Bring food and other necessities to your loved one and to those helping with rescue efforts, if you are able. Your assistance during this time will be greatly appreciated.

6 | Sample Letters to Send to Those Who Are Grieving

A friend is a friend at all times.

Proverbs 17:17

THE NEXT FEW PAGES contain sample letters that were written by the authors to grieving friends and/or relatives. They are presented to give the reader some ideas for writing a letter of condolence. Read through all of them—not just the example that fits your particular situation—before writing your own letter. Keep in mind that what might be appropriate for one person may not be appropriate for another. Circumstances also will play an enormous factor in what you write.

If, after reading through the sample letters, you are still not sure what to write, keep in mind that what really matters is that you are writing a note at all. A simple note that extends your sympathies, that indicates that the bereaved are in your thoughts, and that mentions the deceased will be more appreciated than no note at all.

TO SOMEONE WHO HAS LOST A SPOUSE

Dear Bob,

I was completely overwhelmed when Tom called last night to tell us that Marie had died. We all feel so very bad about her death. Marie was like a sister to me and a dear friend to all of us. Please accept our deepest sympathies and know that our friendship, our prayers, and our love are with you and the girls at this very sad time.

Marie always was willing to give a helping hand, no matter what the circumstances. She loved people, and she loved to help them. But she was more than a thoughtful, giving person. Marie was a good friend. She taught me much about life. I will miss her deeply.

I will always treasure the good times our two families had together. I remember the time we got lost going to the Wisconsin Dells, and Marie kept trying to describe all those exotic but nonexistent points of interest along the way. How we all laughed! That was one of the best times we ever had. Marie may be gone from us physically, but she will never be gone from our hearts or our memories.

I can't begin to know how much you and the girls will feel Marie's loss, but I do know how much she loved and adored you. I know that the days ahead will be very different and difficult. But I hope that your faith, which has always supported and guided you in the past, will somehow help make this tremendous transition just a little bit easier, and perhaps a little less confusing.

I know Marie's family will be staying with you for the rest of this week, so I will call you next Wednesday to talk and to see what we can do to help you and the girls, even if it's just to talk. In the meantime, take care. Our thoughts and our prayers are with you.

Love,

TO AN ADULT WHO HAS LOST A PARENT

Dear Marty,

Our family offers you and your family our deepest sympathy and our prayers on the loss of your mother. We are so sorry for your loss. We know how you honored, treasured, and cared for your mom through her long illness. I realize there are always special bonds between mothers and their children, and I am sure that yours will endure beyond your mother's death.

I can remember all the funny snapshots and videos of you and your parents, that you shared with us. Your family was always dancing and laughing at all your family get-togethers. You had loads of fun and good times. And those good times are still being created by you, your wife, and your son for another generation to enjoy. Tradition goes on. Michael is your pride and joy just as you, Marty, were the pride and joy of your parents' lives. It was a good beginning for Michael to have known the lives of his grandparents in such a loving manner.

The family portraits that hang in your family room will be a special treasure for all of you. Your parents will always be a glance away and just a whisper away in prayer.

I know this is a most difficult time; so much has been asked of you. I truly don't know how you managed these last six months. I know your heart is breaking, and for you we offer our prayers and understanding. Call on us. We're here!

Please allow yourself time to cry and continue to remember the good times you had. In them you will find comfort and strength. May the Lord bless and guide you and surround you with His love.

Love,

TO A YOUNG CHILD WHO HAS LOST A PARENT

My Dearest Robbie,

Today is a very sad day. Your loving dad has died.
You are so young to lose your father. I know that in
the days ahead you will be lonely and miss him very
much. He was such a wonderful man and one of the
greatest dads ever. Everybody who knew your dad is
very sad with you. I wish I could do something to
make your hurt go away.

Robbie, our faith lets us believe that your dad is with
God in heaven, and God knows how much we all will
miss him—especially you! But God has not left you
alone. Your mom is with you, your grandparents are
with you, and your friends and cousins are with you.
They all love you and will help take care of you.

The next couple of days will be very sad and maybe
even a little confusing. Your mom and grandparents
may be crying a lot—you may cry a lot, too. But the
crying means that all of you loved your dad and that
he will be missed. Your mom and grandparents love
you very much and will be there for you. And if you
want to talk to me at any time, just have your mom
call, and we can talk. Maybe you can even spend the
weekend with me sometime, if you want.

Robbie, I wish I could make everything better for
you. But I can't. I do want you to know that Uncle
Bob and I love you very much and that we are sharing the sadness you are feeling about your dad.

Love,

TO AN OLDER CHILD WHO HAS LOST A PARENT

Dear Pattie,

I am so sorry to hear that your mom has died. Even though your mom was sick for such a long time, her death still brings pain to those of us who knew her and loved her. I wish I could make your pain and your sorrow disappear, but I do want you to know that I am thinking of you and that I am sharing your sadness.

Your mom was a very special person who would do anything for anyone. While she helped many people, she was happiest when she was doing things for you—and especially *with* you! I remember how happy and proud she was after you were born. You could see the affection and devotion in her eyes every time she looked at you. As you grew bigger and taller with each passing day, so did her love for you.

No one can take your mom's place. She was very special. You and your mom had good times together, happy memories that I hope you will remember and treasure always. Your mom may have died, but her love for you will never die. You will always have that love and her memory forever in your heart—to love, to talk, and to pray to anytime you want.

Pattie, please know that I am here for you if ever you want someone to talk to. You are in my prayers.

Love,

TO SOMEONE WHO HAS LOST A CHILD

Dear Norm and Kay,

Sue and I were so saddened this morning when we learned that your precious daughter Donna had succumbed to her battle with leukemia. Please know that we share in your pain and loss and deeply wish there was some way to lessen the anguish you must be going through.

What a battle she fought during her brief five years of life. Donna always displayed courage despite the obvious pain she was in. She was brave, beautiful, and full of love. Her memory and her life will be with us forever.

The loss of a child is an ache the heart was never meant to know. There is nothing I can say or do that will bring you consolation. But I do know that Donna could not have been loved more by any other parents. Your friends and relatives knew your sacrifices and your pain, which you tried hard not to let Donna see. All she knew was your unconditional love and affection, the soft touch of your hands, the warmth of your words. I know that your hearts are broken and that being with her when she died was most difficult. But I'm sure she was well aware that her loving parents were there with her during her last moments.

Healing from the death of a child is most difficult and may take much time and patience. May thoughts of Donna and your love for each other sustain you and bring you comfort and strength. Take each day slowly. Cry with each other, talk to each other, hug each other. And try to remember that your friends and relatives are praying for you, weeping with you, and sharing your sadness.

We will call you next weekend to see what we can do for you. You will be in our thoughts and prayers.

Love,

TO SOMEONE WHO HAS LOST AN UNBORN OR NEWLY BORN CHILD

Dear Mary and Jon,

We were very saddened to hear about the miscarriage you suffered last week. Please accept our deepest condolences on your loss. If only there was some way to lessen the pain you must be going through at this sad time.

The loss of any loved one is difficult. But you never got to know your little one. Sadder still, that little one didn't get to know you. How we wish that love could have been experienced firsthand. We know that you had such grand expectations for your baby's future. It breaks our hearts that your dreams and expectations have been so suddenly and cruelly halted.

We are heartbroken for you that it was not to be. May you look into your own hearts for strength and run into each other's arms for comfort. Be there for each other. Cry together, pray together, and support each other. And we will be praying for you that your pain may lessen just a little bit each day.

You are in our thoughts. We will call you next week to see if there is anything we can do for you. If you need someone to talk to before then, please don't hesitate to call. We are here for you.

Love,

TO A COWORKER WHO HAS LOST A FAMILY MEMBER

Dear Evelyn,

At this morning's staff meeting, Mr. Murphy informed us of the death of your father. Everyone was saddened upon hearing the news, for we all knew the closeness between you and your dad.

I would like to extend my personal sympathy to you and your family. I only met your father once—at the company open house two years ago—but I was struck by how proud he was of you and your position within the company. And whenever you spoke of your father, there was always love and respect in your voice.

This must be a difficult time for you and your family. I hope that you will be able to draw upon the strength and courage that you always display at work to help you deal with your loss and your sorrow.

During your absence, Bob and I will make sure that your messages and mail are answered promptly and that your desk isn't swamped with work.

Everyone at work is thinking of you in your time of sorrow and hoping that memories of your father will bring comfort in your time of need.

Sincerely,

TO SOMEONE WHO HAS LOST A LOVED ONE TO SUICIDE

Dear John and Charlene,

Sue and I were shocked and deeply saddened when Aunt Rose called to tell us about Amy's suicide. Our hearts, prayers, and love go out to you at this most difficult time.

I know that there is nothing I can say that will begin to relieve the pain and disbelief you must be feeling. Amy was such a loving and caring person. We will always cherish the fond memories we have of her at so many family get-togethers. Her laughter, warmth, and humor will be sorely missed.

We pray that your faith will bring you comfort, that your strength and determination will bring you consolation and support, and that your wisdom will bring you relief from any and all unwarranted feelings of culpability that might creep into your thoughts. You are great parents whose hearts have been broken. Sue and I both hope that the burden of your grief will lessen as time goes on. May the memories of Amy's life get you beyond the agony you now share and may tomorrow's sunshine and love replace the gloom and heartache of today.

Sue and I want to do what we can to help you during these sad days. I will call next Friday to find out how we can make things a little bit easier for you to bear.

Our hearts and tears are with you.

Love,

TO SOMEONE WHO HAS LOST A LOVED ONE TO VIOLENT OR UNEXPLAINED DEATH

Dear Karl,

I was very saddened and distressed when your dad called to tell me that the authorities had found the body of your friend Terry. I know that you were one of the people who searched for him, hoping he would turn up alive. What a shock it must have been for his family and for you to have this ordeal turn out in the manner that it did. We all want you to know how very bad we feel for you and how sorry we are about your friend's death.

I wish I could offer some words of wisdom that would help make sense of his death, but I can't. I only know that it was his *life*, though brief, that did make sense. In some small way, some special way, his life touched yours and the lives of all his friends, classmates, teammates, and relatives. A flame that once shone brightly has been extinguished, but an ember will flicker in your heart forever as you carry your memories of him with you throughout your life.

Our thoughts and love are with you. Remember you can call on us anytime.

Love,

TO SOMEONE WHO IS FACING THE ANNIVERSARY OF A LOSS

[On anniversary of death]

Dear Bill,

I am writing to say hi and to let you know that you and the kids are in our thoughts. I know that in a few days it will be one year since Marianne died, and I was thinking of how the events of one year ago must be overwhelming for you.

It doesn't seem possible that Marianne has been gone from us for so long. At times it seems that it was just yesterday that I talked to her on the phone. At other times, it seems that it's been so long since I heard her voice. I still miss her so much and can only begin to imagine how much you, Timmy, and Michelle long to feel her touch or hear her voice.

Death may have ended her life but it can never end the relationship we each had with her. In our hearts and memories, Marianne will always be your beloved wife, Timmy and Michelle's loving mother, and my cherished close friend.

Bob and I are always here for you, so please don't hesitate to call—Marianne always said we were good listeners!

Love,

[wedding anniversary]

Dear Bill,

I know that you and Marianne would be celebrating your nineteenth wedding anniversary on Friday, and I wanted you to know that Bob and I have been thinking about the two of you all week. We can recall your wedding like it was yesterday, and fondly remember the love the two of you shared for eighteen years.

We hope you are well and that things are steadily getting better. I will call you on Friday to see how you are doing.

Love,

7 | Support Groups

Those who hope in Yahweh
will regain their strength,
they will sprout wings like eagles.

Isaiah 40:31

Choosing whether or not to participate in a grief support group can be a most difficult decision. Many people know nothing about support groups or what to expect from them. The expertise and encouragement such groups provide make them an excellent means of getting the help you need as you proceed on your journey through grief.

WHEN YOU NEED MORE SUPPORT
THAN YOU'RE GETTING

Many people in grief have the notion that support groups are for extremely depressed people or for "weak" individuals. This is just not true. People who are not depressed or who in fact are quite strong emotionally often need help sorting through their feelings and emotions. Grief is almost impossible to deal with alone. You need to share your feelings; now is not the time to keep your personal problems to yourself.

How will I know when I should go to a support group?

There is no correct time frame as to when you should attend a support group. What might be the right time for one person could be the wrong time for another. Each of us grieves at our own pace and for our own personal reasons. Each one of us has our own set of special situations or issues to work through. But if you have any of the following emotions or thoughts, you should consider a support group:

- "I think I need some help to understand my feelings."
- "Why do I still cry so much?"
- "I can't seem to let go."
- "I'm just not functioning very well."
- "I'm so angry at [the person] for leaving me alone."
- "I'm mad."
- "I think I'm going crazy."
- "I can't sleep at night."
- "I just can't stay at home anymore."
- "No one wants to help me or be around me anymore."

- "My family and friends want me to get help."
- "No one understands me and what I'm going through."
- "I blame God for my loss; I hate him."
- "I've lost my faith."
- "What can I do to make it hurt less?"
- "Why am I so critical of others' happiness?"
- "I still blame myself."
- "I should have been the one to die."
- "Why do other people's words and/or actions offend me so much?"
- "Is there anyone who can suggest books, articles, videos, or seminars to help me through all this?"

If you fit any of these scenarios, you should consider participating in a support group. It can be very cathartic to talk with others who have been through an experience similar to yours.

Where do I find a support group?

More and more bereavement services and grief counselors can be found throughout the country. Funeral homes in particular have taken the lead in making available brochures about grief and in sponsoring support groups. In many instances, funeral homes have teamed up with local churches to build a network from which the whole community can benefit. Contact funeral homes in your area to see what means of encouragement they can offer you.

Many local hospitals have begun their own grief support programs. This can be especially comforting to people who have spent considerable time at the hospital with their dying loved ones. Because they remember the many kindnesses offered by hospital staff, they feel comfortable going back to grief support groups either on hospital grounds or sponsored by the hospital.

Check the yellow pages for bereavement groups, therapists, or counselors. You can also search your medical insurance reference book for groups. You can inquire whether the local government in your township provides bereavement services. Medical facilities and charitable associations are also good resources for finding assistance in dealing with your grief.

What can I expect from a support group?

Don't be surprised if you promise yourself that you will go to a support group—and then don't keep your promise. It is normal to find an excuse not to go. In fact, it may take several trials and "almost made it there" episodes before you actually arrive at your first group meeting.

Once there, you will find that the people are open and very approachable; most likely, there will be one person specified to greet you and every other participant who arrives. You may find a smaller—or larger—group than you expected. The number of people present is not the primary issue. The facilitator hopes that, in any group, at least one person will have his or her load lightened as a result of the meeting.

Most likely, you will be presented with a booklet of handouts and reading materials about grief. In some instances where larger groups are planned (usually in hospitals, which will wait until the potential number of grievers is sufficient to warrant scheduled grieving sessions), there will be a guest speaker who addresses all the participants, after which the audience will be broken down into smaller groups who have experienced similar losses. In smaller bereavement groups, there will be just a facilitator who will chair the meeting. In either instance, you will have the opportunity to hear others with similar stories. You will have the chance to express your own feelings as well.

Are there support groups for children?

Some of the larger support groups, especially those at hospitals, will have separate bereavement sessions for children. These meetings are geared toward children only. Generally, these sessions will be a mixture of discussions about feelings and emotions as well as talking about happy memories and playing fun games to relieve the tension and sadness. The children may be told that it's OK to be sad, scared, and even happy if they believe that their loved one is in a better place and no longer in pain.

Each child may be given the opportunity to meet privately with a grief counselor to discuss feelings. In the group, each child may be asked to partner with another child near in age, and if possible, one who has experienced the same type of grief (death of parent, death of grandparent). Then these two partners will be asked to tell each other about their deceased loved ones and see what things they had in common: they lived in the country, they liked to read stories, and so forth.

Children might be asked to share what they liked most about the deceased. They will be asked to draw a picture of how they felt when the person died and then, to change the pace, a picture of his or her favorite possession. Some groups will then use the pictures to construct a giant quilt. This quilt can then be displayed at a private party for the children and their families, where the children can picnic, play games, and win prizes, with each child receiving his or her own special prize.

Finally, as a gesture of love to the deceased, some support groups will have the children write a letter to their deceased loved ones telling them how much they love them and miss them. These letters might be attached to helium-filled balloons (each child might choose a balloon of the color that was the deceased's favorite) and released into the sky. While each group is different and some may not have the funds to do so much, all will offer assistance to the children in their grief. Children who attend bereavement sessions almost unanimously find it helpful in dealing with their loss.

HOW TO EVALUATE OR ORGANIZE A GRIEF SUPPORT GROUP

The criteria used to evaluate the success of a grief support group can also be utilized to organize your own, should you decide to do so. You can begin a group in conjunction with your church, hospital, or local government; you can convene anywhere that meeting space is available on a regular basis.

What are the goals of a support group?

The purpose of the bereavement support group is to help the participants heal. But there are specific goals that need to be stated in the beginning; these goals should be achieved during the meetings. Specifically, the griever should be able to answer yes to these or similar questions:

- Did I learn techniques to manage grief?

- Did I learn that my feelings of grief may change drastically from one day to the next?

- Was I able to relate to the feelings or experiences of others at the meeting?

- Did I come to understand that my feelings, actions, and responses are normal for a grieving person?

Grief shared with others often helps to lessen the burden. The benefits of attending each session should become increasingly obvious to you. If you find that you are not connecting in any of these ways, this particular group is not meeting your needs. Try to find another group to attend.

What is the job of the facilitator?

While all the people who assist with the grief support group must be professional and exercise discretion at all times, it is the facilitator of the group who can make or break the meeting. He or she has the brunt of the responsibilities and should do the following:

- Start the session promptly.

- Introduce himself/herself.

- Set the meeting guidelines and time frames.

- Stress the extreme confidentiality of the stories and feelings expressed at the meeting.

- Explain that the format used at the meeting is geared toward each participant sharing the exact reason for his or her attendance at the meeting.

- Reassure all participants that they do have a choice between sharing their stories or just listening.

- Explain that all feelings are accepted and not judged.

- Affirm that that all participants are entitled to their own opinions and viewpoints.

- Allow each participant ample time to speak.

- Move the session along if a participant is particularly long-winded.

- Announce refreshment breaks.

- Keep the meeting within the time allowed.

What ancillary materials are helpful for a support group?

Some support groups have a table set aside to display articles, booklets, videos, and other resources that are available for participants to borrow. These displays might be grouped according to age of readers (children, young parents, older widows and widowers), types of long-term care (cancer, heart failure, strokes), or types of death (SIDS, car accident, murder). Funeral homes will often donate small brochures and handouts for the participants. Reprints of newspaper or magazine articles are also helpful. This lending library can be an icebreaker for some, since the participants usually choose one or two booklets or articles that have special interest to them. Larger books about grief are generally not included in this library since most grieving people cannot focus on a large, hard text soon after a death has occurred. However, a list of reading materials about grief and bereavement is usually made available to the group for their personal use.

8 | Closing Thoughts

Blessed are those who mourn:
they shall be comforted.

Matthew 5:5

DEATH—AND GRIEF—are matters of the heart. When a heart is broken, it needs to mend. People must come to terms with the fact that death is both real and final. Death comes, a loved one dies, and grief suddenly takes hold. The overwhelming sadness due to the physical separation from a loved one makes it necessary to mourn.

Grief is complex and individual. All emotions and expressions are legitimate and must be accepted as such. If you are in mourning, it is important to work through your grief. If you are a friend of someone in mourning, it is important to look within yourself and help your friend or relative travel this journey. By listening, caring, using common sense, giving encouragement and reassurance, and sharing honest feelings, you can help the bereaved accept the death of their beloved.

At the completion of a journey through grief, mourners can

- Come to grips with the limitations imposed upon survivors
- Explore not only their concerns, fears, needs, apprehension, confusion, and perceptions about grief but also their expectations at the time of a personal loss
- Resolve any feelings of guilt caused by the stress of the dying process or by any unfinished business, misunderstanding, or unsatisfactory conversation with the deceased

Eventually, through time, work, and determination, the person in grief will achieve some degree of closure. Grief is indeed a journey, one that is never quite finished. But those who must make the journey will pass milestones and arrive at a different place from where they began. The journey itself will provide opportunities for healing and growth.

9 | Other Resources

Behold, we live through all things . . .
Bereavement, pain;
 All grief and misery, all woe and sorrow . . .
     Elizabeth Akers Allen, Endurance

ORGANIZATIONS

Listed below are some organizations that may be of value to you in your journey through grief. The information listed is for the national headquarters of each organization. When you contact these organizations—by phone, mail, or e-mail—you will be given information about the support group nearest you. These are only a few of the organizations and Web sites available. Searches of the words "grief," "support groups," "bereavement," "mourning," and so forth will lead you to numerous other organizations, some of which exist only on-line.

Grieving Spouses

The Beginning Experience International Ministry Center
1657 Commerce Dr., Suite 2B
South Bend, IN 46628
Telephone: 219-283-0279
Web site: http://www.beginningexperience.org

The Widowed Persons Services Program
AARP
601 E Street NW
Washington, DC 20049
Telephone: 800-424-3410
Web site: http://www.aarp.org/griefandloss

Grieving Children

Rainbow Children's Support Groups
2100 Golf Road, #370
Rolling Meadows, IL 60008-4231
Telephone: 800-266-3206
Web site: http://www.rainbows.org

Grieving Parents

Compassionate Friends
P. O. Box 3696
Oak Brook, IL 60522-3696
Telephone: 877-969-0010
Web site: http://www.compassionatefriends.org

SIDS Alliance
1314 Bedford Avenue, Suite 210
Baltimore, MD 21208
Telephone: 800-221-7437
Web site: http://www.sidsalliance.org

SHARE
Pregnancy and Infant Loss Support
300 First Capitol Drive
St. Charles, MO 63301
Telephone: 800-821-6819
Web site: http://www.nationalshareoffice.com

Suicide

American Association of Suicidology
4201 Connecticut Avenue NW, Suite 408
Washington, DC 20008
Telephone: 202-237-2280
Web site: http://www.suicidology.org

Violent Death

Parents of Murdered Children (POMC)
100 East 8th Street, Suite B41
Cincinnati, OH 45202
Telephone: 888-818-POMC
Web site: http://www.pomc.com

Mothers Against Drunk Driving (MADD)
P.O. Box 541688
Dallas, TX 75354-1688
Telephone: 800-GET-MADD (438-6233)
Web site: http://www.madd.org

Loss of a Loved One in the Armed Forces

Tragedy Assistance Program for Survivors (TAPS)
2001 S Street NW, #300
Washington, DC 20009
Telephone: 800-959-TAPS
Web site: http://www.taps.org

Loss of a Pet

Rainbows Bridge
(online memorial services and grief support)
1167 Rte 52 PMB 139
Fishkill, NY 12524
Web site: http://www.rainbowbridge.com

BOOKS

The books below are geared primarily toward children and are sorted by subject. There are many more books in your library and bookstores that can be very useful in your healing journey.

Helping Children Grieve

General

Schaefer, Dan and Christine Lyons. *How Do We Tell the Children: A Step-by-Step Guide for Helping Children Two to Teen Cope When Someone Dies.* New York: Newmarket Press, 1993.

Updated and revised, a step-by-step guide on how to talk to children about death; also explores how their emotions might make them react to their loss.

Ages Three to Nine

Brown, Margaret W. *The Dead Bird.* Illustrated by Remy Charlip. New York: W.R. Scott, 1958.

Through example, how to plan and carry out a funeral for a found bird.

Carrick, Carol. *The Accident.* New York: Seabury Press, 1976.

A beloved pet is killed by a truck. The book teaches readers how to manage guilt, anger, and sadness as well as how to rely on memories to bring joy.

Shriver, Maria. *What's Heaven?* Illustrated by Sandra Speidel. New York: Golden Books, 1999.

A child asks her mother questions about heaven and death when her great-grandmother dies.

Stoddard, Sandol. *Growing Time.* Boston: Houghton Mifflin, 1969.

A young boy copes with the death of his dog and with understanding life.

Viorst, Judith. *The Tenth Good Thing about Barney.* Illustrated by Erik Bleguad. New York: Atheneum, 1971.

An illustrated story about the death of a cat and about the good things said about the pet at his funeral.

Ages Nine to Twelve

Krementz, Jill. *How It Feels When a Parent Dies.* New York: Knopf, 1981.

Interviews with children about their loss and how they are coping.

LeShan, Eda J. *Learning to Say Good-by: When a Parent Dies.* New York: MacMillan, 1976.

For adults on how to explain death to youngsters.

Zim, Herbert Spencer and Sonia Bleeker. *Life & Death.* Illustrated by Rene Martin. New York: Morrow, 1970.

A question-and-answer book for children up to age eleven.

Teenagers

Gootman, Marilyn E. *When a Friend Dies: A Book for Teens about Grieving and Healing.* Minneapolis: Free Spirit, 1994.

Short and to the point for teens in grief, it offers compassion and wisdom, confirms that all feelings are normal, and corroborates that teens and adults grieve differently.

Gravelle, Karen and Charles Haskins. *Teenagers Face-to-Face with Bereavement.* Englewood Cliffs, N.J.: Julian Messner, 1989.

Seventeen young adults share their honest views about the loss of their loved ones.

Grollman, Earl A. and Max Malihow. *Living When a Young Friend Commits Suicide, or Even Starts Talking about It.* Boston: Beacon Press, 1999.

Simple talk about suicide, the book analyzes the grieving process, talks about emotions caused by suicide, and discusses what to do to help someone contemplating suicide.

Grieving the Death of a Parent

Mann, Peggy. *There Are Two Kinds of Terrible.* Garden
City, N.Y.: Doubleday, 1977.

A young boy must cope with the death of his mom as well as a dad who is
unable to relate to him.

Grieving the Death of a Brother or Sister

Donnelly, Katherine Fair. *Recovering from the Loss of a
Sibling.* New York: Dodd, Mead Publishers, 1988.

Explores the psychological aspects of losing a brother or sister, addresses
questions such as "Can this happen to me?" or "Why did it happen to him?" or
"Is God punishing me?", and deals with the fact that the survivors may receive
very little support for their pain, even from their parents.

LaTour, Kathy. *For Those Who Live: Helping Children
Cope with the Death of a Brother or Sister.* Omaha,
Nebr.: Centering Corp., 1983.

Suitable for both children and adults dealing with sibling loss.

Richter, Elizabeth. *Losing Someone You Love: When a
Brother or Sister Dies.* New York: Putnam, 1986.

How sixteen people from adolescence to age twenty-four felt when their
siblings died and how they coped with their losses.

Grieving the Death of a Child

Berezin, Nancy. *After a Loss in Pregnancy: Help for
Families Affected by a Miscarriage, a Stillbirth, or the
Loss of a Newborn.* New York: Simon & Schuster,
1982.

Talks about dealing with your loss.

Davis, Deborah L. *Empty Cradle, Broken Heart: Surviving
the Death of Your Baby.* Golden, Colo.: Fulcrum
Publishers, 1991.

Offers encouragement and advice for dealing with the loss of a baby.

Friedman, Rochelle, and Bonnie Gradstein. *Surviving Pregnancy Loss: A Complete Sourcebook for Women and Their Families.* Secaucus, N.J.: Carol Publishing Group, 1996.

Revised and updated, it offers valuable advice for mothers, fathers, and their families in dealing with ectopic pregnancies, stillbirths, and miscarriages.

Grieving Widows and Widowers

Brothers, Dr. Joyce. *Widowed.* New York: Simon & Schuster, 1990.

Dr. Brothers shares her journey through grief describing her emotions, loneliness, and pain and how she was able to move forward.

Caine, Lynn. *Widow.* New York: Morrow, 1974.

One woman's courageous journey of healing.

Campbell, Scott and Phyllis R. Silverman. *Widower: When Men Are Left Alone.* Amityville, N.Y.: Baywood Publishing Company, 1996.

Establishes that men do grieve differently than women and offers the stories of how twenty men successfully overcame their pain and shock at the death of their spouse.

Grollman, Earl. *Living When a Loved One Has Died.* Boston: Beacon Press, 1997.

Written simply, it offers advice and comfort for those who have sustained a loss.

Jones, Jane Griz. *From Grief to Gladness: Coming Back from Widowhood.* Baltimore, Md.: Recovery Communications, 1999.

Suggestions for women and men on dealing with grief and how to help their recovery.

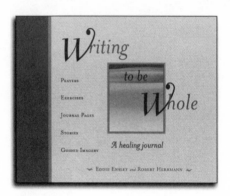